40.25

Digital Typography Pocket Primer

By Ron Goldberg

Portions of this book are adapted from *Practical Typography* by Frank J. Romano and used with permission.

Requests for permission or further information should be addressed to:
Permissions Department
Windsor Professional Information, LLC
11835 Carmel Mountain Road, Suite 1304
San Diego, CA 92128

This and other books in this Pocket Primer series are available at special quantity discounts for use as premiums and sales promotions, or for use in corporate training programs. For more information, please contact:
Special Sales
Windsor Professional Information, LLC
11835 Carmel Mountain Road, Suite 1304
San Diego, CA 92128
858-487-2945   Fax: 858-487-3279
e-mail: windsorpub@earthlink.net

This publication is designed to provide accurate and authoritative information regarding the subject matter covered. However, the author and publisher make no representation or warranties of any kind with regard to the completeness or accuracy of the contents herein and accept no liability of any kind, including but not limited to performance, merchantability, fitness for any particular purpose, or any losses or damages of any kind caused, or alleged to be caused, directly or indirectly from this book.

Library of Congress Cataloging-in-Publication Data
On file with the Library of Congress
ISBN 1-893190-05-6

Printed in the United States of America
First edition   A B C D E

Credits:
Copy Editor: Phyllis DeBlanche
Production Management: LUX Design, San Diego
Cover Design: Douglas Hyldelund

Contents

This book is dedicated to my parents. Without their love and support, I never would have had the chance to push myself and reach my goals. Their special love and understanding made me what I am today.

Special thanks also go out to my friends Elana, Jason, Rich, and Tony, who dealt with me on those long nights I stayed up working, as well as to Joanna, who has supported me and has always been there through the good and the bad times.

Most importantly, though, thanks to those at Rochester Institute of Technology, where I found my true love for the printing industry. Those who helped to make this book a reality include Marcia Carroll, Grace Gladney, Archie Provan, Dick Spayde—and Frank Romano. Without his support and belief in me, this book would not have been possible.

Ron Goldberg
May 1999

1

Digital Fonts

Typography is the arrangement of letters and spaces on a surface, whether it is paper or on a monitor, to communicate information and facilitate understanding. Typographers are people who look at letters and their shapes and forms and color when combined into words and pages and documents, and think about their history and their future. Although calligraphers are not usually considered typographers, the history of typography must begin with calligraphy, for this was the beginning of written communication.

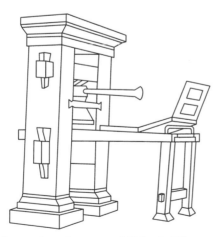

When Gutenberg invented printing from movable type, he had knowledge of character shapes, spelling, page layout, and metal engraving, and this knowledge was based on the books available to him, which were handwritten by monks and other scribes. Attractive layout, practical page proportions, the amount of text on a page, line length, margins, and other artistic approaches had long since been established. His goal was to mass-produce books that looked as though they had been written by scribes.

Metal-to-film-to-bits

Type today is based on early handwritten letters or a modification of early typefaces, which were modeled after calligraphic lettering in manuscripts. Roman lowercase letters and capitals kept their current form until 1470, in a face created by Nicholas Jenson. Typefaces designed after Jenson's typeface were used in manuscripts, and those similar to it are called Venetian type.

Phoenician	Early Greek	Classical Greek (Ionian)	Early Latin	Classical Latin
alph		alpha		A
beth		beta		B
gimel		gamma		C
daleth		delta		D
he		epsilon		E
		digamma		F
				G
heth		eta		H
		iota		I
				J
kaph		kappa		K
lamed		lambda		L
mem		mu		M
nun		nu		N
ayin		omicron		O
pe		pi		P
qoph		qoppa		Q
res		rho		R
sin		sigma		S
taw		tau		T
				(U)
		upsilon		V
waw				W
		chi		X
yod				Y
zayin		zeta		Z
		omega		
		theta		
samekh				

The evolution of the alphabet is the quest to write faster and faster.

Print began as chunks of metal, way back when Johann Gutenberg invented movable type. The pieces of type were kept in large cases with compartments for each letter, called typecases. The lower part of the typecase held the lowercase letters, while the upper part held the capital letters (in the upper case). Letters or symbols could be selected and placed next to each other in a type or composing stick, and a thin piece of lead was placed on top as a line spacer when the line was complete. The lines were then transferred to a larger type tray called a chase, and this was repeated until a complete page was assembled, made up of thousands of pieces of metal.

Points were used to measure the length of each metal chunk of type. A 72-point H, in metal type, is a character cast on a metal block, and the block's top surface or typeface is, for example, exactly 72 points (1 inch) in height. The actual character when printed will usually be smaller than the overall size of the metal, which is necessary because of the ascenders and descenders. In order for the type to line up squarely, each character must be cast onto the metal blocks, which are large enough to allow the ascenders and descenders to project above and below the baseline. In the end, all the characters end up being the same height, which determines the point size of the typeface.

Even before point sizes were used, each individual size was given a name, but by the 1800s it was realized that it was too difficult to distinguish between one size and the one just below it if there were different names; thus, a man named Nelson Hawkes developed the point system and used numbers to describe type sizes. Lettering first consisted of all capital letters, but with the increase in demand for printed material, scribes tended to writer faster, and this evolved the lowercase style. To do so, they created lettering with more fluid motions of the pen. This eventually was translated into the design of typefaces.

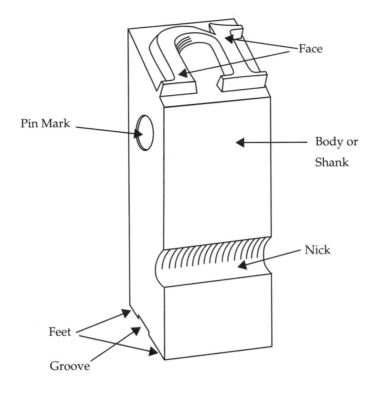

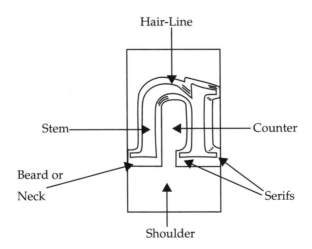

Example of metal type, with parts shown.

In the nineteenth century, the idea came about to find a way to create a machine that would set type automatically. Many machines were created with the intention to replace hand typesetting, but the first was by Dr. William Church, in 1822. None were built well enough to stand up to commercial work, though, until 1886 with the invention of the Linotype by Ottmar Mergenthaler.

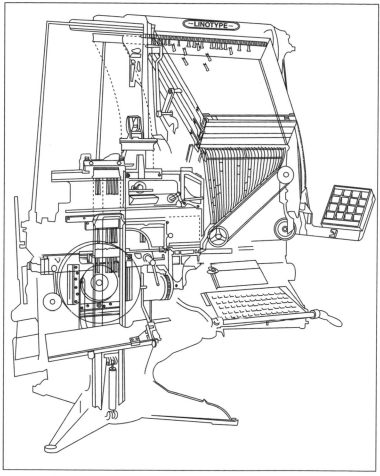

Mergenthaler's Linotype.

One of Mergenthaler's problems was that of automatic justification. The answer was the patent for the variable wedge that was held by

J. W. Shuckers. The Linotype Company eventually bought the company holding the patent, and there was no serious competition for years to come. The basis of the Linotype was to set a line at one time.

In 1887, the Monotype was invented by Tolbert Lanston. This machine was made of two parts, a keyboard and a caster. Each letter was cast separately and justified manually. When a key was tapped, it perforated a paper ribbon. Once the ribbon was punched, it was placed on the caster, and compressed air was passed through the holes to position a case containing matrices over a mold. The combinations of punched holes positioned the case to cast a specific letter and adjust the mold width to suit the unit width of the character. Each character was cast and delivered into a tray.

After new technology was introduced, metal type soon faded away as methods for creating type on film became possible. The invention of photographic typesetting is what made this all possible. The traditional point measurements with metal type were a hindrance for this new method of setting type. It was not possible to use the actual height of the letters and measure them in inches or millimeters. For phototypesetting, there were three ways to size the type:
- Each photo matrix had a different master size, and characters were reproduced 1:1.
- Photo matrix had one master size, and lenses were enlarged or reduced to the character image.
- Photo matrix included a variety of master sizes, and each side was enlarged to create a range of sizes.

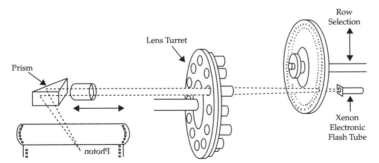

A typical photographic typesetting system.

Some suppliers made their master sizes all the same size and worked from constant-size artwork. So, all typeface art would be 7 inches high and reduced to the 8-point master size. In many cases, this effectively eliminated the x-height variability, and all the sizes were the same. With digital type, the letters are now made up of thousands of dots, overlapped to create lines (called rasters), which has increased the number of sizes possible.

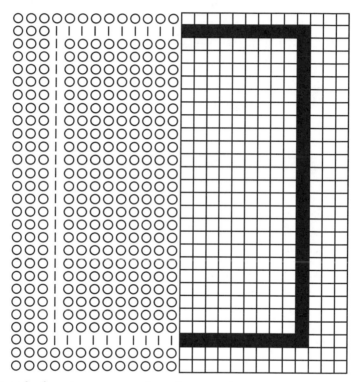

Example of a raster, as zeroes and ones become spots.

So as technology was introduced, the number of sizes possible increased. We went from about 15 to 20 sizes from 6 to -72 point to between 1,000 and 10,000 sizes from 5 to 500 point. Today you have any size in three-decimal increments from 5 to 500 point.

Here we demonstrate one-decimal-point increments. Note how difficult it is to discern the difference in size. However, it is helpful in getting type to fit a given space.

Agxh Agxh Agxh Agxh Agxh Agxh Agxh Agxh Agxh Agxh									
12.0	12.1	12.2	12.3	12.4	12.5	12.6	12.7	12.8	12.9

abcdefghijklmnopqrstuvwxyz   12.0-point
abcdefghijklmnopqrstuvwxyz   12.1-point
abcdefghijklmnopqrstuvwxyz   12.2-point
abcdefghijklmnopqrstuvwxyz   12.3-point
abcdefghijklmnopqrstuvwxyz   12.4-point
abcdefghijklmnopqrstuvwxyz   12.5-point
abcdefghijklmnopqrstuvwxyz   12.6-point
abcdefghijklmnopqrstuvwxyz   12.7-point
abcdefghijklmnopqrstuvwxyz   12.8-point
abcdefghijklmnopqrstuvwxyz   12.9-point

Point size differences do not look that different when placed next to each other, but the line-length difference shows that something is happening.

PostScript
In the early 1980s, Adobe Systems developed a way to describe typographic images as vectors, or outlines. This gave type an elasticity that allowed more sizes and variations from the same electronic image. Before that, type for digital output was stored as bitmaps—sets of dots—for each typeface and point size. At the same time, they invented a page-description language called PostScript, which was made up of more than 300 verbs and commands that could describe type and pages, fill boxes, select typefaces, etc. The third thing they needed to design was something to interpret this new format, and they created a PostScript interpreter or raster image processor (RIP).

When the RIP receives the PostScript file, it needs to convert it to bitmapped data. PostScript printers use the interpreter to translate the PostScript code into the bitmapped information needed to print a file. The RIP plots out the page as a grid of spot locations. All spots can be located based on the x and y coordinates it sits on. The image can be thought of as having a spot or not having a spot (1 or 0). When only two values are used, it is called binary.

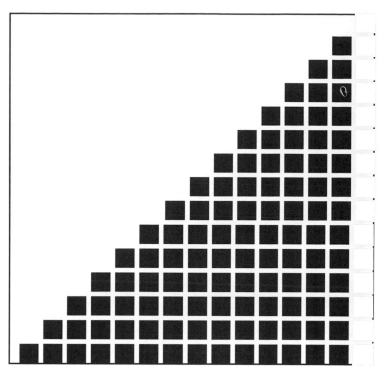

Raster image processors convert the outline data into spots in a grid.

PostScript is a page-description language and is expressed as plain text. PostScript is commonly used for both line art and text. In the former, it is often referred to as Encapsulated PostScript (EPS). An EPS is a PostScript file with a preview. There are two EPS types: ASCII, which is text-based, and binary, which is hexadecimal. Vector-based programs that allow the user to save in EPS format usually use the ASCII format.

In the EPS ASCII format, there are two versions of the graphic. One version is the resolution-independent PostScript description for printing on a PostScript device. The other is a low-resolution bitmapped PICT preview that can be displayed without using PostScript interpretation. With this feature, page-layout programs like QuarkXPress can import, crop, and scale graphics while using the PICT image. If there is no PICT file attached to the EPS, the application will display a gray box.

When saved as an EPS, the file cannot be ungrouped, refilled, or recolored. The only functions that can be done are recropping, resizing, and adding distortion. Most programs that do any color separations accept EPS files since they are self-contained.

Binary EPS is similar to ASCII versions, containing the PICT preview and the actual graphic. The difference is that instead of saving the file as a PostScript description file, it saves it as a list of numbers that represents pixels. Binary EPS files are used very successfully for outputting bitmapped color images for four-color separation.

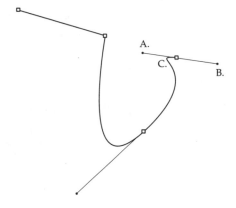

It starts with a Bézier curve.

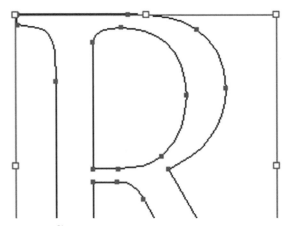

It becomes an outline.

The interpreted character is then filled and converted to spots.

PostScript Type 1 fonts are compressed, since they require only one file to create all sizes of a single type style. To display these fonts the Macintosh needs the outline, a 10-point bitmapped (screen) font of the typeface, and Adobe Type Manager (ATM). The outline file contains information required to render the typeface, and the information is encrypted. PostScript Type 1 uses Bézier mathematics to describe the shape of the curve. This type of math uses fewer control points to extrapolate the outline of the letters.

Hints maintain the look of type when printing below 600 DPI and in type below 14 point. Hints include making sure all the letters line up, creating visually accurate curves and strokes, and adjusting overall quality. A hint may shift a letter so that it fits in with the other letters that are near it. Font manufacturers are the ones that control hinting, and not all fonts have the capability to use it.

PostScript Level 2 was created in 1990. In 1998, Adobe announced the release of Adobe PostScript Level 3. The big change in this version was to allow customers the ability to print complex graphics and Web content, when and where they needed it. With new digital technologies, Level 3 was created to support digital document creation processes. With enhanced image technology, documents print faster, with optimal quality. PostScript Level 3 also supports direct processing of Web content, including HTML and PDF.

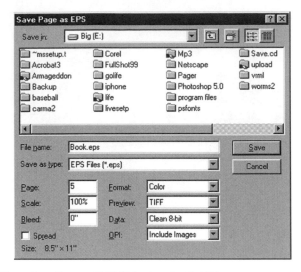

QuarkXPress Save Page as EPS dialog box for the PC.

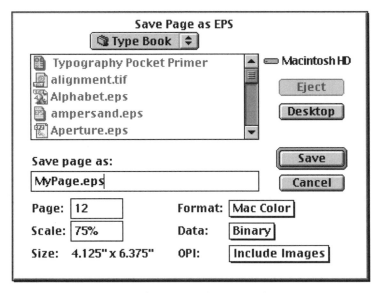

Saving a page as EPS in QuarkXPress on the Macintosh.

Word-processing and editing programs are able to open a Post-Script file, and with knowledge of the syntax of the language, the user could go in and edit the text. All PostScript files begin with

%!PS, which informs the program or RIP that it is a PostScript file. Any lines with a % in front of it are there only to comment.

The comments are found in the beginning of the file, and for a simple letter R, look like this:

```
%!PS-Adobe-2.0 EPSF-1.2
%%Creator: QuarkXPress(R) for Windows 4.0
%%Title: Document1 (Page 1)
%%CreationDate: 3/14/99 7:54 PM
%%DocumentProcSets: QuarkXPress_EPS_4.0 3.0 1
%%DocumentSuppliedProcSets: QuarkXPress_EPS_4.0 3.0 1
%%DocumentFonts: ArialMT
%%DocumentData: Binary
%%LanguageLevel: 1
%%BoundingBox: 0 0 612 792
%%EndComments
```

The rest of the code fills thirteen, 8-1/2x11-inch Quark pages. A sample of the beginning of the code is as follows:

```
/c1 0 def/m1 0 def/y1 0 def/k1 0 def
/cstp 0 def/mstp 0 def/ystp 0 def/kstp 0 def
/blmode 0 def
/blf 0 def
/blstp 0 def
/blw 0 def
/minblnd 16 def
/mtx matrix def
/T true def
/F false def
/B{bind def}bind def
/X{exch def}B
/m/moveto load def
/l/lineto load def
/rl/rlineto load def
/p2{pop pop}B
/p3{pop pop pop}B
/p4{pop pop pop pop}B
/setcustomcolor where{pop/docust{save 1 index 4 get
  [.5 .5 .5 0 6 -1 roll] 1 setcustomcolor currentgray
  exch restore dup 1 eq exch 0 eq or}B}{/docust{F}B}ifelse
/setseparationgray where{pop/doregblnd T def/sepgr{setseparationgray}B}
  {/doregblnd F def/sepgr systemdict/setgray get def}ifelse
/setsepval{dup -1 eq{pop aload pop setcmykcolor}
```

There is no need to have the program with which the PostScript file was created to print it. A PostScript file can simply be sent to the RIP, and the RIP will be able to print the document. Once the file is saved as a PostScript file, it is not possible to edit it unless you know PostScript and can change the code using a word processor, text editor, or know a geek who will do it for you.

PostScript fonts also exist, and were created after TrueType fonts. Both TrueType and PostScript fonts are scalable. Bézier curves are used to create characters in PostScript fonts. A PostScript font for the Macintosh is made up of the suitcase containing the screen fonts (bitmaps) and the printer fonts. Screen fonts allow for maximum legibility on the screen of the fonts. For the Macintosh there are many different icons that stand for a PostScript file, and each file has three things that make it up. These things are the NFNT resource, the FOND resource, and the printer outline font. These three things are necessary for a PostScript font to be read by the computer.

The NFNT resource takes the bitmap for each character and stores it. The FOND resource controls everything the user sees about the font including the name, point size, formatting, etc. It also links all the bitmaps, printer fonts, and suitcase files together so that they can be used properly and ensure proper printout. Finally, the printer outline font contains all outline data needed for the Bézier curves, and also includes any hinting that may be used for the particular font.

To use PostScript fonts in Windows, Adobe Type Manager (ATM) must be installed, since the only fonts that Windows allows a user to install are TrueType fonts. The PostScript fonts are made up of a PFB and a PFM file. The PFB file is what allows the user to see the fonts on the screen correctly, as well as allows the fonts to print correctly on the page. This file also holds all the Bézier data, as well as any hinting instructions that may also be added to the font. The PFM file contains all the other instructions and information for the font, such as kerning pairs, spacing values, etc.

As long as you are using ATM for PostScript fonts, there will be no problem printing to a non-PostScript printer.

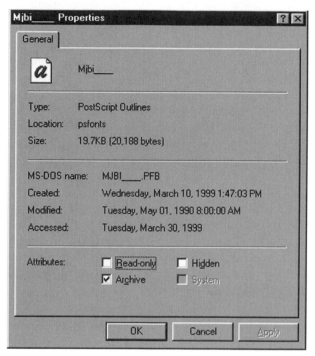

Information box for a .PFB file.

When using PostScript fonts, though, it is more efficient to print to a PostScript printer, since the job will print in a shorter amount of time. It is possible to convert fonts from TrueType to PostScript if there is a need to do so. The problem with doing such a conversion is that it will not always be done with accuracy. There is really no pressing reason that a font should need to be converted from True-Type to PostScript since printers can read the TrueType format whether it is a PostScript or non-PostScript printer.

TrueType
From late 1987, Apple had been developing what was to become TrueType. At that time there were many competing font scaling technologies, and several would have been suitable for the Macintosh. It was by no means certain, according to lead engineer Sampo Kaasila, that Apple would adopt TrueType. In the end though, it proved itself on performance and rendering quality (at high and low resolution) against the others. Kaasila completed his work on

TrueType, though it didn't yet have that name, in August 1989. The following month, Apple and Microsoft announced their strategic alliance against Adobe, where Apple would do the font system and Microsoft the printing engine. Apple released TrueType to the world in March 1991—the core engine in much the same form that Kaasila left it back in 1989. Microsoft introduced TrueType into Windows with version 3.1 in early 1992. Working with Monotype developed a core set of fonts that included TrueType versions of Times New Roman, Arial, and Courier. These fonts showed, just as Apple's TrueTypes had, that scalable fonts could generate bitmaps virtually as though each size had been designed by hand.

With non-fancy fonts, the system generally worked well. However, since Windows 3.1 had to run on machines with slow 16-bit 286 processors, the TrueType system had to be reconfigured as a 16-bit implementation of Kaasila's fundamentally 32-bit architecture. Memory allocation did not work all of the time, though it did on occasion. There were major problems with the PC version of True-Type. One major flaw was that complex characters would some-times fail to display at all, or they'd appear on screen but not on the printer. Only in August 1995, with the release of Windows 95, did Microsoft's TrueType engine become 32-bit, which allowed True-Type to be used in the form in which it was created. Now it features grayscale rasterization (anti-aliasing), which makes the text on the screen look much nicer than before.

These fonts can be used for both the screen display and printing, thereby eliminating the need to have two font files (screen and printer) for each typeface. This format uses square B-spline mathe-matical formulas (Quadratic) to extrapolate type outlines. Using these formulas allows the computer to create the characters at any size or resolution.

In other words, the fonts are scalable and use many control points along the character. TrueType fonts use hinting. *Hinting* a font is a method of defining exactly which pixels are turned on in order to create the best possible character bitmap shape at small sizes and low resolutions. Since it is a glyph's outline that determines which pixels will constitute a character bitmap at a given size, it is often necessary to modify the outline to create a good bitmap image. This modification changes the outline until the desired combination of pixels is turned on. A hint is a mathematical instruction added to the font to distort a character's outline at particular sizes.

On the Macintosh, TrueType fonts are made up of the SFNT resource and a FOND resource. These two resources are combined into one file that contains all the data to create the characters. Originally designed to work on non-PostScript printers, they work on PostScript printers as well. When looking on the Macintosh at a list of fonts, the TrueType fonts do not have a number for point size after them. These fonts must be stored in the Fonts folder on the Macintosh, unless a font manager is being used. In the PC format, TrueType fonts have the extension of TTF. All TrueType fonts are located in the Fonts folder (Windows 95 and 98), although if a font-management program is used, they may be stored in a folder outside the font folder. Any fonts which have an icon of a blue-and-gray T on the PC platform are True Type fonts.

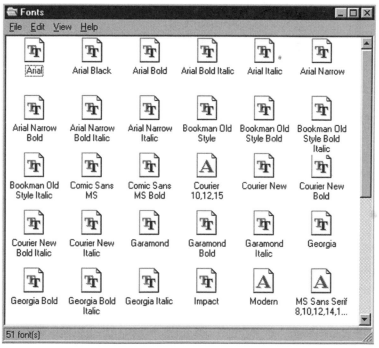

Screen shot of the Fonts folder on the PC.

New fonts can be installed by opening the Fonts folder, clicking on the start menu, and then choosing control panel.

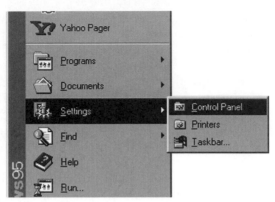

Control panel as seen when opening it from the Windows start menu.

Once the control panel window is opened, the font folder can be opened by double-clicking it.

Control panel expanded on the PC.

The new fonts can then be installed by choosing Install New Font under the file menu.

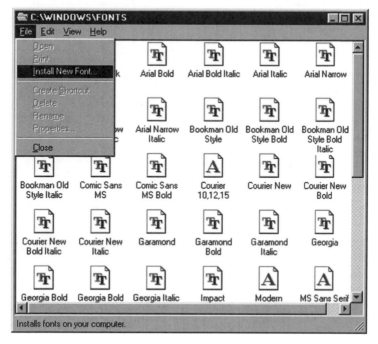

Font menu with Install New Font highlighted for installing TrueType fonts.

By browsing and choosing the font, it will be automatically installed and added to the font folder.

Notice that there is the capability to take fonts off a network, if there is network capability.

These fonts can then be shared by other users on a network, in case of missing fonts.

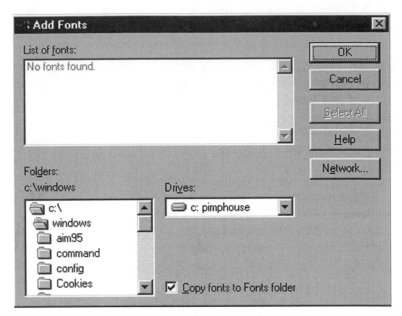

Browsing window on the PC to locate new fonts to be installed.

To remove a font, the user just needs to choose the font and delete it out of the Fonts folder. The user will be asked if they are sure that they want to delete the file and would proceed by clicking on the Yes button.

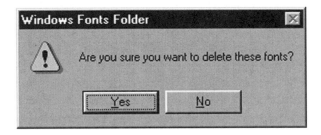

Windows dialog box to ensure deletion of a file.

Windows 95 and 98 also allow the user to preview the font by double-clicking on a certain font from the Fonts folder. This preview gives the user the name, file size, version, copyright information, examples of all the characters, and examples of point sizes that are available.

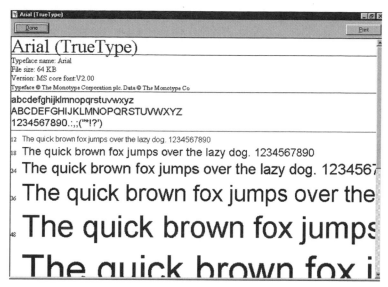

Typeface sampler in Windows.

Font sample on Macintosh.

On the Macintosh, fonts are loaded by simply dragging them to the Fonts Folder in the Extensions Folder in the System Folder, or using a font utility to load fonts as needed.

The Macintosh Fonts folder.

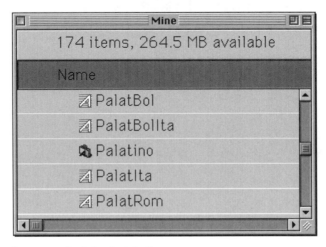

You need screen and printer fonts both.

Screen fonts used to come in sizes, but ATM negates all except 10 point.

One of the most important things about fonts is to make certain that when you install them, there is not another font with the same name. It does not matter if it is a different format, such as a Post-Script font. If a TrueType and a PostScript font are installed on the system with the same name, it will cause problems for the user. There should be no problem printing on any printer, since Post-Script printers print TrueType fonts—the operative word being "should." When using a PostScript printer, TrueType fonts will print much slower, since RIPs are designed to handle fonts in the PostScript format.

There may sometimes be a need to convert fonts from PostScript to TrueType format. The main reason this would need to be done is when a user does not have ATM but would like to use a PostScript font. ATM is not expensive, and costs about $40, and will allow the user to use PostScript fonts. If the user so chooses, there are programs that will help convert fonts from one format to an other. Examples of these include Macromedia Fontographer and Ares FontMonger, which is no longer sold.

The fonts that come installed with Windows 95 are as follows:

Font	Version
Arial	2.00 (WGL4)
Arial	2.00 (Win ANSI)
Arial Bold	2.00 (WGL4)
Arial Bold	2.00 (Win ANSI)
Arial Bold Italic	2.00 (WGL4)
Arial Bold Italic	2.00 (Win ANSI)
Arial Italic	2.00 (WGL4)
Arial Italic	2.00 (Win ANSI)
Courier New	2.00 (WGL4)
Courier New	2.00 (Win ANSI)
Courier New Bold	2.00 (WGL4)
Courier New Bold	2.00 (Win ANSI)
Courier New Bold Italic	2.00 (WGL4)
Courier New Bold Italic	2.00 (Win ANSI)
Courier New Italic	2.00 (WGL4)
Courier New Italic	2.00 (Win ANSI)
Marlett	1.00
Symbol	1.00
Times New Roman	2.00 (WGL4)
Times New Roman	2.00 (Win ANSI)
Times New Roman Bold	2.00 (WGL4)
Times New Roman Bold	2.00 (Win ANSI)
Times New Roman Bold Italic	2.00 (WGL4)
Times New Roman Bold Italic	2.00 (Win ANSI)
Times New Roman Italic	2.00 (WGL4)
Times New Roman Italic	2.00 (Win ANSI)
Wingdings	2.00

Fonts installed with Windows 95.

Fonts that come installed with Mac OS:

Times
Courier Regular
Helvetica
Symbol
Chicago
New York
Geneva
Monaco
Palatino
Charcoal (added to Mac OS 8)

Fonts installed with the Mac OS.

There are different sets of fonts installed with ATM depending on the version. Version 4.0 Deluxe comes with the following:

Caflish Script Regular and Bold
Critter
ExPonto Regular
Lithos Regular and Black
Minion Ornaments
Minion Condensed Regular, Italic, Bold, and Bold Italic
Myriad Tilt
Myriad Roman, Italic, Bold, and Bold Italic
Nueva Roman, Bold Extended
Poetica Chancery 1
Tekton Multiple Master Roman and Oblique
Sanvito Roman and Light
Utopia Regular, Italic, Semibold, and Semibold Italic
Viva Regular and Extra Bold Condensed
Willow

Fonts installed with ATM 4.0 Deluxe.

Note: This is as good a place as any to warn you about PostScript and TrueType fonts living in the same folder. Sometimes—many times—they will not print properly when used in the same document. Since almost all RIPs are PostScript RIPs, we suggest sticking with PostScript Type 1 fonts.

Fonts that come with ATM 3.8 and 3.9 include:

Times Roman, Italic, Bold, and Bold Italic
Courier Regular, Oblique, Bold, and Bold Oblique
HelveticaRegular, Oblique, Bold, and Bold Oblique
Symbol
Berthold Baskerville Regular, Italic, Medium, and Medium Italic
Boton Regular, Italic, Medium, and Medium Italic
Poppl-Laudatio Regular, Italic, Medium, and Medium Italic
ITC Anna
Boulevard
Giddyup
Giddyup Thangs
Tekton Multiple Master

ATM Version 3.8 and 3.9 fonts.

Microsoft products also come with a selection of additional fonts, for both the applications and the Web. The standard fonts with these applications are shown on the next page.

Adobe Minion Web
Andale Mono (formerly Monotype.com)
Arial
Arial Black
Comic Sans MS
Courier New
Georgia
Impact
Times New Roman
Trebuchet MS
Verdana
Webdings
Marlett
Symbol
Wingdings
Lucida Sans Unicode
Lucida Console
Tahoma

Common fonts that come with Microsoft products.

Font troubleshooting
Fonts are still a problem area if you are not vigilant. Here are some of the common font issues:

Characters are okay on the screen but don't print right.
- You're probably using a Postscript font. The screen font is okay, but there is a problem with the printer font. Make sure you installed the two files.
- On old Macintosh system versions, the two files must be in the same folder to work properly.
- If you're using a TrueType font, the file may be corrupted. Install it again from the original disk, or redownload.

Characters are italicized or bold on screen but not when printed.
- Slanting a normal font is not recommended. First, an

italic is different from a slanted version; most typefaces have italics drawn very differently. It is the same for bold versions; bolding a font makes it regularly thicker, when the real bold versions are generally more thick horizontally than vertically.

• In those two cases, you won't obtain something typographically right. Added to that fact, most programs can't really do it. They allow you to slant a character on the screen, but when it's printed, they replace it with the bold version of the font, if it is available in the font file. If no bold or italic versions are available, the normal version is printed.

Characters are bitmapped on screen (i.e., they are not drawn smoothly but with big squares).

• You're probably using a PostScript font, and there is probably a problem with the screen font. Make sure you installed it with the printer file. On old Macintosh system versions, the two files must be in the same folder to work properly. (This does not occur if you're using ATM, which calculates the screen font size using the PostScript file.)

• If you're using a TrueType font, the file may be corrupted. Reinstall it from the original disk, or redownload it from its source.

• Characters are bitmapped at large point sizes. ATM needs more memory, so it cannot smooth out the characters. Increase the amount of memory allocated to the "character cache size" on the ATM control panel. If you can't, or if still it is not enough, reduce the number of fonts currently loaded.

When you select a font, another one appears. Or it appears, but with odd spacings or leadings.

• This is an example of font conflicts, which are slowly becoming extinct. What is called a font conflict is in fact a font ID conflict. Fonts have two kind of IDs: their name and an integer value, its ID number. Until recently, most programs were identifying fonts with their integer value.

- If you had two fonts that have the same ID (two public-domain fonts, for example, for which their authors haven't asked Apple for a personal number), those programs were confused about the appropriate font to use.
- The only solution is to change the font ID, and a lot of utilities have been issued to do so. One can also use programs like Fontographer or Font Studio. Since Suitcase and ATM 4.0 are automatically dealing with this problem, and with most of the recent programs using the font's name instead of ID number, font ID conflicts are becoming less and less frequent.

Text is printed in Courier instead of the PostScript font on your screen.
- This is due to the fact that someone changed the name of the PostScript file of the font you're using and your computer is not able to find it, and it replaces it with the default font—Courier. The best thing to do is to trash the corrupted file and replace it with a new copy or the original version. Or you do not have the printer font—just the screen font—and PostScript sets the default font. This is known as silent substitution because it happens with no alert to warn you that it is happening.

Bézier
Bézier refers to mathematical equations commonly used to describe the shapes of characters or graphic images in electronic typography. The points on the curve are not actually on the curve itself. The Bézier curve was named for Pierre Bézier, a French computer scientist who developed the mathematical representation used to describe the curve B-spline. It is used in PostScript, where a minimum of four points are required to define a curve.

By moving and turning a set of handles, the curve can be changed. Most commonly, the use of Bézier curves is found in programs like Adobe Illustrator and Macromedia FreeHand (as well as in QuarkXPress 4 and Adobe InDesign), where curves are used for drawing purposes.

The illustration on the next page shows a letter G defined by a set of Bézier curve points.

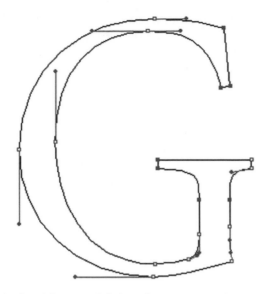

Example of a Bézier curve defining a letter.

Quadratic

Quadratic curves are used with TrueType fonts where only three control points are required, with all points on the actual curve.

Line art created in rich detail with Bézier curves.

Multiple master

Adobe came out with multiple masters in 1991. This enables a user to create additional fonts from two or more master designs within a single typeface family. Think of multiple masters as being totally elastic—they can be stretched horizontally and vertically to create typographic variations. With the application Font Creator for the Macintosh, which is provided with each multiple master font, a custom font can be stored in the System Folder or in a folder outside the System Folder. In Windows, the ability to use multiple master fonts is built into Adobe Type Manager. The user has the ability to adjust a maximum of four attributes: weight, width, optical size, and style. Not all fonts allow a user to have control of all four attributes, though.

> *Weight* controls the stroke weight, from light to bold.
>
> *Width* controls the width of characters, from condensed to extended.
>
> *Optical size* controls optimal legibility, which includes fixing of serifs if too light.
>
> *Style* can be controlled in only certain typefaces, and varies by definition depending on the typeface.

Agxh	TektoMM
Agxh	TektoMM 100LT 250CN
Agxh	TektoMM 100LT 564NO
Agxh	TektoMM 100LT 850EX
Agxh	TektoMM 240RG 250CN
Agxh	TektoMM 240RG 850EX
Agxh	TektoMM 503BD 250CN

In the typeface TektoMM, a wide variety of combinations can be created. In this example, the LTs stand for light, CN is condensed, EX is expanded, RG is regular, and BD is bold.

For example, style could control serifs from sans serif to serif or wedge to hairline. The name of the typeface will have an MM after it to indicate that it is a multiple master font. The numeric design will also be listed such as the following: 350 wt 500 wd 10 op, as seen above.

In Windows, the only way to create other versions or instances is to do it in Adobe Type Manager (ATM). To do this, click on the base multiple master font and click on the Add Fonts tab. Once the Add Fonts window pops up, pull down the source window and change it to create multiple masters.

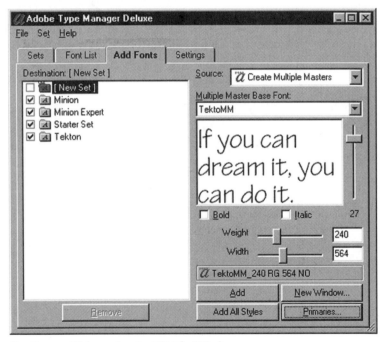

Creating multiple masters in ATM for Windows.

Upon changing the pull-down window to create multiple masters, the screen above will appear. In the window, there are many options. Right under the preview window are the words "italic" and "bold." Upon clicking in either of those boxes, the font will then take on that appearance. The other two controls are weight and width.

Weight moves on a sliding scale of 100 to 620, and width works on a scale of 250 to 1100. Once you have created a typeface and want to keep it, click the add button and it will place it on the font list.

Like all other fonts on the PC, the font is listed in the font list unless it is unactivated by the user.

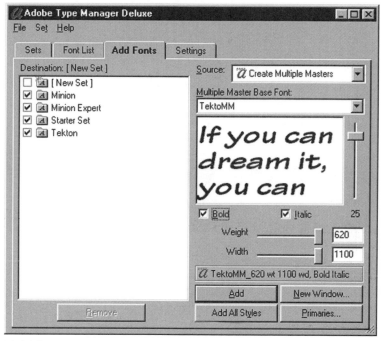

Multiple Master set up in ATM (Adobe Type Manager), with all characteristics set to the maximum, for the PC.

The same thing can be done using Adobe ATM for the Macintosh. The screen is a little different, but the same changes can be made for a typeface, as well. The fonts that are created will be listed in the font list.

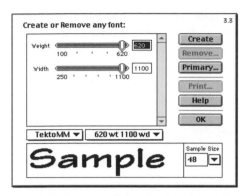

Mac multiple master dialog showing the maximum setting.

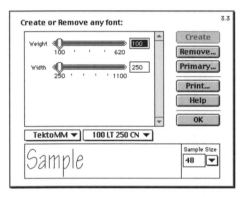

Mac multiple master dialog showing the minimum setting.

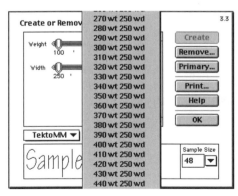

Each version is then listed as a separate font.

Bitmaps

Bitmaps are a matrix of individual dots or pixels that make up the graphic display. Each pixel corresponds to bits in the processor's memory. Lines are built up as rows of adjoining pixels, or pixel elements. Bitmaps are used mostly for screen display and printing on old dot-matrix printers. To create a smooth transition between two colors that may be near each other, dithering is used. Dithering looks at the pixels of color or gray that are in one row, looks at the color or grays in another row, and averages the two rows to create a third between them.

Black and white bitmaps only need one bit to describe them, either a 0 or a 1. When expressing a color, there must be more than 1 bit to represent the color. Images containing 256 grays or colors require 8 bits per pixel, and photos require 24 to specify any of 16.7 million colors.

Bits	Colors
6	64
8	256
10	1,024
12	4,096
24	16.8 million
30	1 billion
36	68 billion

Resolution, color, and grayscale determine the tremendous size some bitmaps can become. Low-resolution bitmaps will print out at a low resolution even if printed on a high-resolution printer. When bitmaps are enlarged, they emphasize the jaggedness that makes them up. Bitmapped fonts work in tandem with outline fonts, with bitmap fonts being used on the screen and connected outline fonts automatically used in the printer. Various paint programs deal with images as bitmaps.

Bitmaps can be confusing because the term is also used for:

- Fonts that are produced at a fixed size and style and are incapable of being resized. This format is not used anymore except for really weird fonts downloaded from Web sites.
- The result of the raster image processing process, where every laser dot is placed on a grid for the imaging engine indicating whether the dot is on or off.

Vector
Vectors are object-oriented graphics typically produced by drawing programs. Vectors overcome any limitations that bitmaps have. These images are objects and paths that are described mathematically. Every stroke is saved as a list, so that the program knows how it was created.

Since the strokes are described mathematically, the object can be enlarged, reduced, rotated, shifted, and refilled. Each stroke is able to be moved freely or covered by another object without erasing any part of the original stroke. So vectors are like placing each stroke on a transparent sheet, that can be moved around without disturbing any of the other strokes.

When printing, vectors also have an advantage. Vector images describe where the strokes should be placed, instead of telling the printer where to place each pixel. So vectors are resolution-independent, and if you print an image on a 2,500-DPI imagesetter, it will look far superior than if it were printed on a 300-DPI laser printer, or an ink jet printer.

Bitmaps vs. vectors
Bitmaps are individual pixels in fixed locations. If a bitmap is enlarged, the pixels grow, and the jaggedness becomes quite apparent. When printed, the image retains its jaggedness, regardless of the printer resolution.

Vectors are object-oriented images that consist of mathematically defined paths and drawing instructions. These paths can be rendered sharply at any size or orientation. This allows printers to print at the highest printer resolution possible.

QuickDraw GX

Apple's QuickDraw GX is an updated version of QuickDraw, the language that controls the Mac OS display and printing. Quick-Draw GX enhances printing and font handling and supports color management software. The QuickDraw GX environment handles graphics, typography, and printing differently than does the Post-Script language. As a result, some applications that use PostScript or generate PostScript when printing (e.g., Adobe PageMaker) do not support QuickDraw GX. To make use of all the features available to QuickDraw GX, an application must be "GX-savvy," or written with the intention of running in the QuickDraw GX environment. For information on whether a particular application is GX-savvy, refer to the application's documentation.

QuickDraw GX is included with Apple Mac OS 7.5 and later as well as with some printing utilities, such as Pierce Print Tools. Though it is included with Mac OS software, its installation is optional. It is not installed by default.

To support QuickDraw GX TrueType fonts, applications must recognize their extended character set, which includes up to 65,000 characters per font, and their line-layout capabilities for text composition. QuickDraw GX-compatible applications automatically handle kerning, justification, special characters, proper use of swash and standard characters, morphing for weight and width, and formation of fractions and ordinals (e.g., superscripting "nd" in "2nd,"or "3" in "2 to the 3rd power").

PostScript Type 1 fonts must be "enabled" to work with Quick-Draw GX. Enabled fonts include an SFNT resource containing scalable PostScript outline data and the font's icon with three As, but it does not contain extended characters and advanced features incorporated into QuickDraw GXfonts. Since enabled fonts and True-Type standard fonts both use three As for their icon, you will be unable to determine the font type by viewing its icon at the Finder.

QuickDraw GX automatically provides support for TrueType fonts, but to use enabled PostScript Type 1 fonts, you must use ATM or SuperATM 3.7 (in System 7.x), ATM 4.02, or a later version. Note that installing ATM 4.02, which is included with QuickDraw GX version 1.1.6, replaces any other version of ATM on your system, including ATM Deluxe.

The QuickDraw GX installer for System 7.x automatically enables existing Type 1 fonts located in the Fonts folder in the System Folder. The original Type 1 suitcase and outline font files are moved to the Archived Type 1 Fonts folder; and enabled fonts are located in the Fonts folder.

To disable QuickDraw GX permanently, remove it using the Apple Installer's Custom Remove option. To disable QuickDraw GX temporarily, use Extensions Manager to turn off the QuickDraw GX extensions, or use the QuickDraw GX Helper extension (System 7.x only) to turn Desktop Printing off for specific applications. If running System 7.x or running System 8.x and you used the Type 1 Enabler, remove the enabled fonts and reinstall the original Type 1 fonts located in the Archived Type 1 Fonts folder.

QuickDraw GX was a great effort, but users did not support it. Today the goal is a font format that is cross-platform and cross-media—one that can be used for print and for the Web. Actually, it has been the Web that is driving the push for a new approach to fonts standardization.

OpenType
OpenType is Microsoft and Adobe's collaborative attempt to "end the font wars," unifying the competing formats of TrueType and Type 1 fonts (including multiple masters). It's basically TrueType Open, an advanced, somewhat GX-like version of TrueType with more controls over glyph substitution and placements but with the ability to contain Type 1 outlines.

In practice, it's likely that good TrueType-OpenTypes will be preferred on screen, while Type 1-OpenTypes will work better on old PostScript devices. OpenType uses the same advanced glyph substitution and layout features introduced in TrueType Open ligatures will finally have support at the system level. OpenType fonts will also have a "digital signature," which aims to prevent casual modification to the font.

If someone has ATM, it will use the Type 1 outlines. If not, these will be converted to TrueType, the way WindowsNT has used Type 1 fonts for years. OpenType will be an important standard, but the question is when. WindowsNT will be the first OS that supports the full standard, and the next version of Windows will follow.

Font security problems mean that many type designers will not support this method. This could mean fewer fonts to choose from. Apple has not been forthcoming about their support or lack thereof, but they have other things to worry about. Their next-based OS uses Display PostScript and obviously has close ties to Type 1 fonts the way they are. This could possibly create problems for Apple users.

OpenType includes two kinds of font compression, depending whether there's TrueType or Type 1 data inside. For TrueType, it uses Agfa's lossless font compression technology, MicroType Express (be warned that the claimed 90 percent "compression" is largely due to a font subsetting capability). On the Type 1 side, Adobe's new "Compressed Font Format" averages a claimed 45 percent reduction without subsetting.

OpenType, an evolution of TrueType Open, has a file structure just like TrueType: a series of tables indexed by a table directory. Most tables are formatted identically, no matter whether the actual glyph descriptions are in the TrueType or Type 1 format. If it's Type 1, there is a "typ1" table instead of the "glyf" table.

The following data types are used in the OpenType font file. All OpenType fonts use Motorola-style byte ordering (Big Endian):

Data Type	Description
BYTE	8-bit unsigned integer
CHAR	8-bit signed integer
USHORT	16-bit unsigned integer
SHORT	16-bit signed integer
ULONG	32-bit unsigned integer
LONG	32-bit signed integer
Fixed	32-bit signed fixed-point number
FUNIT	Smallest measurable distance in the em space
F2DOT14	16-bit signed fixed number with the low 14 bits of fraction
LONGDATETIME	Date represented in number of seconds since 12:00 midnight, January 1, 1904. The value is represented as a signed 64-bit integer
Tag	Array of four units (length = 32 bits) used to identify a script, language system, feature, or baseline
GlyphID	Glyph index number, same as unit16(length = 16 bits)
Offset	Offset to a table, same as unit16 (length = 16 bits),NULL offset = 0x0000

Data types for Open Type.

2

Managing Fonts

Macintosh and Windows
Fonts can be stored in various ways on or off the computer:
- On a disk, whether it is a 3½-inch, Jaz, Zip, etc.
- Every time the computer boots up, there are fonts which reside in the system and load ready to go. These are the fonts stored in read-only memory (ROM). Fonts, when being used and activated using one of the programs discussed below, are stored in random access memory.
- Fonts are also stored in most raster image processors on hard disk or in read-only memory.
- In almost every case, fonts are stored at the level of the operating system and are thus available to almost every program.

Screen fonts
Screen fonts are used for computer screen display and contain the bitmaps used to display the font. Screen fonts sometimes look fine at the resolution of the screen (72 DPI on the Macintosh) but are of too low a resolution to be sent to a high-quality output device. In almost all cases, printer fonts are used to send vector-based outlines to the printer.

Printer fonts
Printer fonts can be downloaded to the printer, onto a hard disk or in ROM (read-only memory) that resides in the computer. Some fonts are used more often, and in some environments, it could save time to have them already residing in the ROM of the printer. Fonts can be manually downloaded to the printer; doing this allows them to stay there until the printer is turned off or reset. In the long run, this can help save time since in the duration of a single day it may have been downloaded a few dozen times; only to be downloaded once each day if done manually. Without printer fonts, when printing to an output device, the resolution may be low since all that is available is the screen font bitmap to print from.

PostScript printers usually store the following base fonts in ROM:

Courier
Courier Bold
Courier Bold Oblique
Courier Oblique
Symbol
Helvetica
Helvetica Bold
Helvetica Bold Oblique
Helvetica Oblique Times Roman
Times Bold Italic
Times Italic
Zapf Dingbats

PostScript fonts usually stored in ROM.

RIP (raster image processor)
Raster image processor is the hardware and software that is used with output devices to determine what value each pixel or spot should receive. The RIP is driven by commands from a page-description language. It converts fonts and graphics into raster im-

ages, which are used by the printer to draw onto the page. A memory bit set to "1" means to print the corresponding output pixel as black (on), and a "0" means to leave it white (off). The RIP creates a dot-for-dot representation of the page, which is ready to be printed.

Downloading
Laser printers and other output devices receive data from the computer, such as the file to be printed and the fonts that are needed to print the document.

Downloadable fonts
Downloadable fonts are font files containing character descriptions that are copied from the computer and temporarily stored in the printer's memory while a document is printing. If you want to manually download fonts to your printer using the Macintosh platform, Adobe Systems has created a product called Downloader. With the PC platform, there is usually a utility that comes with your printer, but if not, there are two shareware programs—Psdown and Winps—that will allow you to download printer fonts.

ATM (Adobe Type Manager)
Adobe Type Manager is a program that improves screen display by imaging fonts directly from their Type I PostScript language font files to screen bitmaps. This includes TrueType as well as Adobe-standard Type 1 fonts. It allows a user to print PostScript fonts to a non-PostScript printer. Without this program, it is not possible to scale fonts on the screen. ATM also lets you remove your fonts (Type 1, TrueType, or bitmaps) from the System Folder's Fonts folder and store them on any hard disk. You can then use ATM to activate suitcases or sets (groups of fonts used together) as needed.

Fonts that are used all the time should be placed into a folder that will be activated all the time. Fonts that are used a little less frequently should be placed in a separate folder, and only be enabled when needed. Fonts can be classified in a variety of ways, from the job they are for, to the type family or vendor.

Fonts load into system memory only when they're activated, so if you've got a large font collection, you can reduce an application's RAM requirements significantly by activating only those fonts you need for a particular project. ATM Deluxe also resolves problems with corrupted or conflicting fonts.

Adobe Type Manager's Add Fonts menu.

Since PostScript files cannot be installed onto a PC without ATM, knowing how to use it is very important. When installing the program, the user will be asked to choose a location to store all the fonts on the hard drive. The default location is in a folder called psfonts. It also asks for a default location for all the .PFB and .PFM files, which hold the information for the PostScript fonts, as well as a default location for the TrueType (TTF) fonts. In ATM, a starter set is what is activated all the time. This starter set should have all the fonts that are commonly used in most applications by the user.

The user then, as with most other file management programs, can create other folders by name of font, vendor, job, etc. These folders are activated by clicking a box or deactivated by clicking again and removing the check that signifies that the set is activated. ATM also creates a font list, so that the user can see the full list of fonts at any time and know which ones are activated. To add fonts, ATM uses the standard Windows Explorer to find the fonts and quickly add them to an existing set, or even to create a new set of fonts. To make things easier, fonts can be double-clicked in the font list, so the user can see the same preview that would have appeared by double-clicking on the font name in the font folder.

In order to install PostScript fonts on the PC, do the following:

If the fonts are on a disk, you should insert the disk into the computer and open the ATM program.

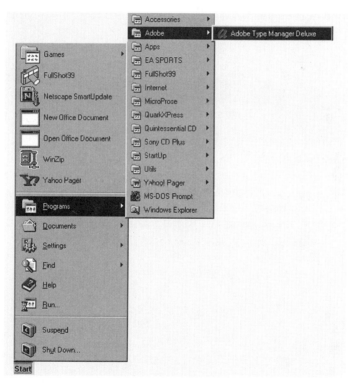

Opening Adobe Type Manager from the Start menu in Windows.

Click on the Add Fonts tab in the ATM dialog box to bring up the following screen:

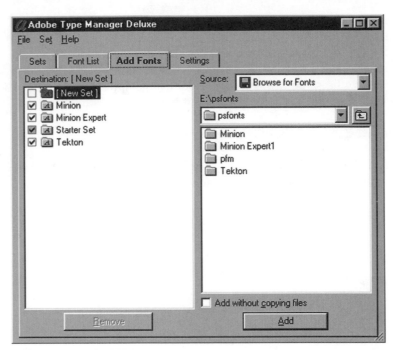

Add Fonts menu in ATM.

Once that tab is clicked, find the destination where the fonts are located. In this example, since they are located on the floppy drive, the source location was changed to the 3½-inch A drive.

Browsing the window in ATM to find new fonts to be installed.

Once the correct drive is chosen, the list of fonts will be made available. Click the ballot box next to the words New Set. A new folder will be created, and the user will be asked to enter a name for the folder. In this case it is named "Sample."

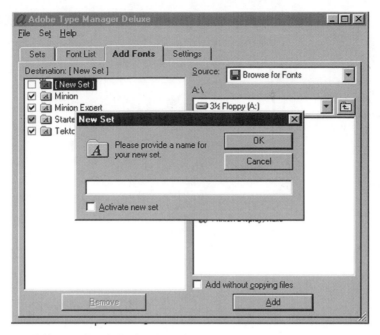

New folder creation dialog box in ATM.

By clicking on the first font that you want and then holding down the control key, you can select multiple fonts that you want placed in the folder.

Upon clicking the last folder, hold down the mouse button and drag the fonts to the new folder that was created. This copies the fonts into the folder.

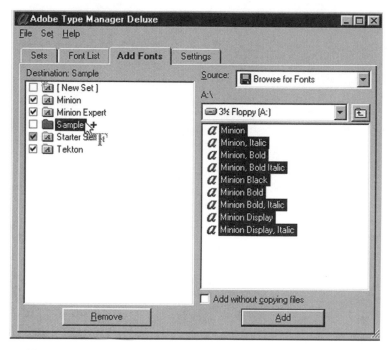

Highlight and drag all new fonts into the folder where they belong.

Once all the files are copied, double-clicking on the new folder will show all the fonts that were installed.

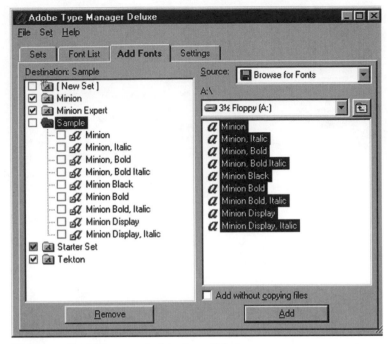

Clicking on the folder expands it to show all fonts.

To activate the font folder, single-click next to the folder name in the
ballot box, and it will activate all fonts in that folder. If you only
want to activate certain fonts, click the ballot box next to the individual font names.

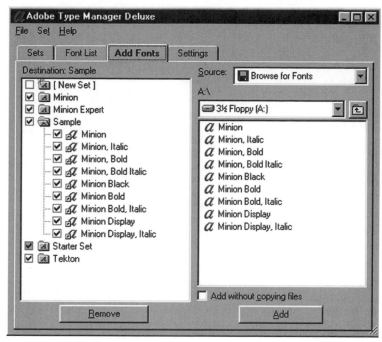

Clicking the ballot box beside the folder activates all fonts in the folder.

To remove a folder or font set, click on the folder name and then the Remove button.

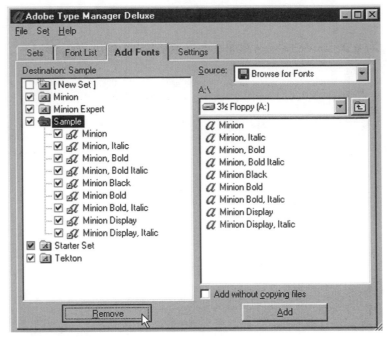

Highlighting a folder for removal from ATM.

You will then be asked to verify that the folder should be removed.

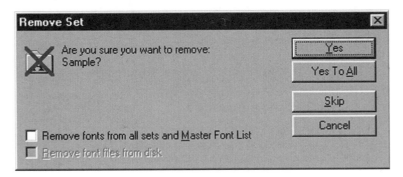

Dialog box that assures deletion of a folder in ATM.

Clicking Yes will remove the fonts and the folder. If you make a mistake and delete any of the sets, they will have to be reinstalled again.

Suitcase

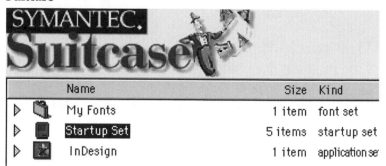

The main window of Suitcase 3.

The program called Suitcase opens "suitcases," or groups of type-faces, when needed, keeping others closed when not needed. Suitcase lets users load fonts as needed from any drive, local or remote. It also allows the user to see the typefaces on the screen exactly how they will print. For the Macintosh, this program is an extension, which is placed in the System Folder. It also has the ability to import and export font ID files for applications that still rely on font IDs. To use Suitcase, all the user needs to do is open it; a box that looks like the above will appear.

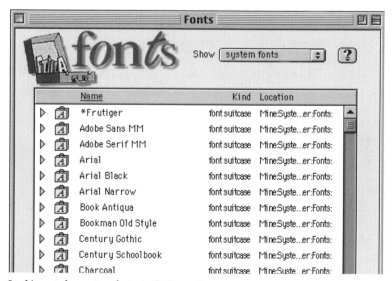

Looking at the system fonts in Suitcase 3.

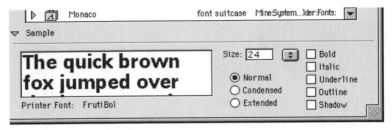

From within Suitcase, you can see a sample of the font.

It is possible to create a folder that holds all the fonts for a specific job. The user will need to create and name a new folder for the job. If for some reason the user decides that only a few of the fonts in a folder need to be activated, the user has the capability to selectively choose what will be added. This program has a problem with crashing, which may mean that the software has to be fully re-installed more than once.

MasterJuggler

MasterJuggler Pro lets you create font sets that can be opened or closed in one step, freeing you to organize your fonts in your own folders, anywhere on the hard drive, and it resolves font-ID conflicts. This program is an extension for the Macintosh that gets placed in the system folder. The program creates two types of sets: startup sets that open automatically when you boot, and temporary sets, which the user can open as needed.

Temporary sets normally close when you shut down, but if your system crashes, when the computer is restarted MasterJuggler will reopen any temporary sets that were active. MasterJuggler also will alert the user if the associated printer font is not available for the screen fonts being used in a document, as well as allow the user to print a catalog of the fonts on the system easily.

The most useful feature of this program is that it allows the user to create sets. Sets are a number of fonts that are going to be placed in a folder because they either belong to a certain job, or all the fonts fit into a certain classification. These fonts can span many folders. Once the sets are created, the user then has the ability to go in and edit the sets, in case a font is removed or not used.

3

Glyphs: A Cast of Characters

A glyph is a symbol used in writing or written communication; a letter, punctuation mark, or figure. A character set, on the other hand, is a single font's characters, and numbers.

ASCII

ASCII stands for American Code for Information Interchange, a computerized numbering scheme used to represent text characters. ASCII does not contain any graphics or special character formatting. There are two types of ASCII codes: 7- and 8-bit. In 7-bit ASCII there are 128 characters; 8-bit ASCII consists of 256 characters or control codes. In each, there are either 7 or 8 bits per character. The letter A is represented in 8-bit ASCII as 01000001, though it is stored as ASCII 65. The letter "B" is stored as 66, "a" as 97, and "b" as 98, etc. Other codes do not create letters but control display, like carriage returns. ASCII 8 is the backspace, for example. The ASCII extended character set ranges from 128 to 255. These characters do not always print consistently. The main purpose of the code is to provide compatibility between devices, since plain ASCII can be read by just about any program. ASCII has been adopted as a standard by the United States government. In the Macintosh platform, there are generally shortcut keys to print the simple characters on the screen. On the PC platform, it is more complex, since the user has to know the correct Alt commands. For example, to print a ™ on the PC, the user needs to key in alt-0153, while the Macintosh operator can use option-2. There are many charts available to help the user create all the special characters needed in typesetting.

In the PC format, if there is not a chart available, the character map can be used to find special characters. The character map must be installed on the system when Windows is installed; otherwise, you will need to reinstall Windows in order to use it. The character map is available by selecting the Start menu, moving to Accessories, and then choosing Character Map.

Selecting Character Map from the Start menu.

In this window, you choose the font that you are working in, and this will show you all the available characters. Upon selecting a letter, the bottom right-hand side of the dialog box will tell you what combinations will create the character.

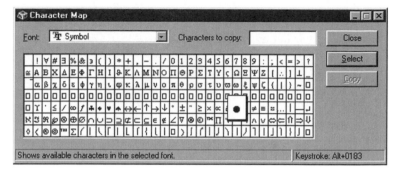

Character Map in Windows.

The character can then be copied by double-clicking it—placing it in the Characters to copy box, highlighting it, and then clicking copy. An easier way to get the character is to use the command given to create the character. It is not advised to use the bullets listed in the character map, since they may have compatibility problems with other Windows applications and especially in Macintosh applications if the file is to be transferred between platforms at some point. The best way to create a bullet is seen in the chart below. Some common characters that are used in typesetting, with their key combinations for the PC platform, are listed on the next page.

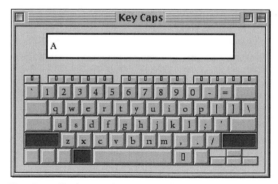

Key Caps display on the Macintosh.

Character	Example	Key combination
Ellipsis	…	Alt-0133
En dash	–	Alt-0150
Em dash	—	Alt-0151
Bullet	•	Alt-0149
Opening double quote	"	Alt-0147
Closing double quote	"	Alt-0148
Opening single quote	'	Alt-0145
Closing single quote	'	Alt-0146
Trademark symbol	™	Alt-0153
Copyright symbol	©	Alt-0169

Special characters on the PC.

There are other ways to create these characters in certain programs, like QuarkXPress, which are discussed later throughout the book.

Key Caps for the Macintosh.

```
Geneva 14
  ! " # $ % & ' ( ) * + , - . / 0 1 2 3 4 5 6 7 8 9 : ; < = > ? @ .
X Y Z [ \ ] ^ _ ` a b c d e f g h i j k l m n o p q r s t u v w x .
ë í ì î ï ñ ó ò ô ö õ ú ù û ü † ° ¢ £ § • ¶ ß ® © ™ ´ ¨   ≠ Æ Ø ∞ ±
... À Ã Õ Œ œ – — " " ' ' ÷ ◊ ÿ Ÿ / € ‹ › fi fl ‡ · , „ ‰ Â Ê Á Ë È
```

One of the most useful utility programs for the Mac is PopCharacter. The icon appears in the upper left corner of your screen and lets you select a character or a symbol by just moving the cursor to a glyph and releasing the mouse button.

On the Macintosh, there are other key combinations that are used to create special characters. In the apple menu, there is a program called Key Caps, which serves the same purpose as character map for the PC.

With Key Caps, the user can see the layout of the keyboard. By pressing shift, option, option-shift, or the control keys, Key Caps will show what characters are available.

These characters can then be double-clicked, highlighted, and copied onto the clipboard to be used in a document. To create the same characters in the chart above on the Macintosh, follow the chart:

Character		Key combination
Ellipsis	...	Option-;
En dash	–	Option-hyphen
Em dash	—	Shift-option-hyphen
Hyphen	-	Hyphen
Bullet	•	Option-8
Opening double quote	"	Option-[
Closing double quote	"	Shift-option-[
Opening single quote	'	Option-]
Closing single quote	'	Shift-option-]
Trademark symbol	™	Option-2
Copyright Symbol	©	Option-g

Special characters on the Mac.

An example of an ASCII table can be found on the next page. On the PC, a nonstandard character (that is, a character not normally found on the typewriter key set) is created using a four-digit number using decimal notation.

For instance, using the table provided, AIT0058 would output a semicolon.

ASCII TABLE

Dec Hex Char	Dec Hex Char	Dec Hex Char	Dec Hex Char
0 0 NUL	32 20	64 40 @	96 60 `
1 1 SOH	33 21 !	65 41 A	97 61 a
2 2 STX	34 22 "	66 42 B	98 62 b
3 3 ETX	35 23 #	67 43 C	99 63 c
4 4 EOT	36 24 $	68 44 D	100 64 d
5 5 ENQ	37 25 %	69 45 E	101 65 e
6 6 ACK	38 26 &	70 46 F	102 66 f
7 7 BEL	39 27 ’	71 47 G	103 67 g
8 8 BS	40 28 (	72 48 H	104 68 h
9 9 TAB	41 29)	73 49 I	105 69 i
10 A LF	42 2A *	74 4A J	106 6A j
11 B VT	43 2B +	75 4B K	107 6B k
12 C FF	44 2C ,	76 4C L	108 6C l
13 D CR	45 2D -	77 4D M	109 6D m
14 E SO	46 2E .	78 4E N	110 6E n
15 F SI	47 2F /	79 4F O	111 6F o
16 10 DLE	48 30 0	80 50 P	112 70 p
17 11 DC1	49 31 1	81 51 Q	113 71 q
18 12 DC2	50 32 2	82 52 R	114 72 r
19 13 DC3	51 33 3	83 53 S	115 73 s
20 14 DC4	52 34 4	84 54 T	116 74 t
21 15 NAK	53 35 5	85 55 U	117 75 u
22 16 SYN	54 36 6	86 56 V	118 76 v
23 17 ETB	55 37 7	87 57 W	119 77 w
24 18 CAN	56 38 8	88 58 X	120 78 x
25 19 EM	57 39 9	89 59 Y	121 79 y
26 1A SUB	58 3A :	90 5A Z	122 7A z
27 1B ESC	59 3B ;	91 5B [	123 7B {
28 1C FS	60 3C <	92 5C \	124 7C |
29 1D GS	61 3D =	93 5D]	125 7D }
30 1E RS	62 3E >	94 5E ^	126 7E ~
31 1F US	63 3F ?	95 5F _	127 7F DEL

Punctuation

One of the first printers to break up text with punctuation was Aldus Manutius, before 1500. There was inconsistent use of punctuation before Gutenberg's invention of movable type. The period was used for a full stop at the end of a sentence, and the solidus was used as a comma, to indicate a pause. The semicolon was introduced in the late 1500s in England.

The apostrophe is used in contractions and abbreviation or to form possessives. In some cases, an apostrophe should be added to avoid ambiguity: "A's were all over my report card."

Additional space at the ends of sentences is called French spacing, and is common of books printed throughout the nineteenth century. In typesetting, a thin space set in addition to the word space achieves French spacing.

Another way to use punctuation is hanging punctuation. Hanging punctuation places the punctuation in the margin, so optically the text appears to be justified. In the Gutenberg Bible, the hyphens were hung in the margin, so it is not such a new idea after all. New programs, like InDesign, apply optical spacing approaches.

The comma that is in use today used to be a slash. It was introduced in England in 1521, in roman type, and 1535 in blackletter. It can be seen in Venetian type printed before 1500. The question mark has been in use since 1521 in England.

Semicolons are first seen around 1569 in England, but this character was not commonly used until 1580. The period or full stop was commonly used before the roman and sometimes also with arabic numerals until 1580. Finally, the opening single quote and the closing single quote were used indifferently in abbreviations, such as th' for the. Also, using 't'is' instead of 'this was common.

The following is a list of common punctuation marks that are used to indicate correct pronunciation and to otherwise assist in making composition clear and understandable:

,	Comma	´	Acute accent
;	Semicolon	^	Circumflex accent
:	Colon	¨	Dieresis/Umlaut
.	Period	¸	Cedilla
–	En dash	" "	Quotation marks
—	Em dash	...	Ellipsis
?	Question mark	*	Asterisk
!	Exclamation point	†	Dagger
()	Parentheses	‡	Double dagger
[]	Brackets	§	Section
'	Apostrophe	¶	Pilcrow
-	Hyphen	{}	Braces

Commonly used punctuation marks.

Symbols

Symbols, signs, and ornaments appear in typefaces and are not letters. These also include marks representing words, monetary symbols, mathematical symbols, and flourishes. Some are designed to match a font, while others may be included in a separate symbol or pi font.

Pi fonts are collections of special characters. The name pi originally came from handset metal type, where *pi* referred to one style of type mistakenly put in the storage drawer of another style. When setting type, a composer may have run across a letter that did not match the face being used. This "orphan" would then be thrown into a box of pi type, called a hell box, to be sorted out later or sent back to the type foundry for credit when reordering a new font. Pi was also a form of type that had collapsed or spilled, and was usually attributed to the printer's devil: the apprentice.

The best way to view the characters available in one of these fonts is to use either the character map or Key Caps, depending on which platform you are using. Ornament fonts are not always included. You can automatically access the symbol font by pressing the following key combinations:

PC: control + shift + Z
Mac: command + shift + Q

An example of a symbol font is Wingdings:

Pi referred to characters or symbols that were inserted by hand. On the Linotype, these symbols did not run in the magazine like other characters and were inserted by hand, and then came down the "pi chute" and were stored in the pi tray.

When handset type was arranged into lines and then dropped by accident, the resultant mess was said to be "pied."

On the Macintosh, the Symbol font and Zapf Dingbats are the most commonly used pi fonts.

Equations and math
Mathematical symbols are frequently used in documents. The symbols used are single letters used to designate unknown quantities, variables, and constants. They should always be set in italic type, except vectors, which should be set in bold.

Numerals, operators, and punctuation are not italic, nor are trigonometric functions or abbreviations. Items set in plain type should always be preceded and followed by a space. Examples follow on the next page:

log 2 *not* log2

What to do and not to do when setting mathematical equations.

When creating more complicated mathematical equations, brackets should be used.

$$\sin \ [2p(x\text{-}y)/n]$$

Correct use of brackets in equations.

Mathematical equations should always have a space before and after the operators that have numbers on both sides.

4 x 5 cm

Correct spacing used before and after operators.

When using plus and minus signs that are not part of an equation, there should be no space between the sign and the number. An en dash should be used instead of a hyphen for a negative sign.

–12 C

Correctly used en dash for the negative sign, with no space used between the sign and the numeral.

When using mathematical expressions, they can be a sentence only if the subject, verb, and object are a part of the expression, as in this example:

When $V = 12$, then eq 15 is valid.

Mathematical expression used as a sentence, which contains a verb, subject, and object as a part of the expression.

In regular body text, the equal sign (=) should not be used to replace the word "equal" in a sentence. This also applies to greater than (>) and less than (<) symbols as well as for the plus (+) and minus sign (–). The only time a space is not left before and after numerical operators is when they are subscripts or superscripts.

When equations are listed on separate lines, they should be numbered with arabic numbers in parentheses placed in the right margin. If the equation is short and will not be used again, it should run in to the text without being numbered. When using the solidus to show division, and you cannot tell where the numerator starts or the denominator ends, parenthesis should be used to make it more clear. Whenever using multiple sets of parenthesis, square brackets should be used on the outside. When needing three sets, use braces around the square brackets.

$$\{34+2[9*786(345/4)]\}$$

Proper use of parenthesis, brackets, and braces in mathematical equations.

Italic type is used for single letters that denote mathematical constants, variables, and unknown quantities in text and in equations. When single letters become adjective combinations, they are still italic. Chemical element symbols used to denote attachment to an atom are set in italic type. Italic letters within square brackets are used to form names for polycyclic aromatic compounds. In polymer nomenclature, *co*, *alt*, *b*, *g*, *r*, and *m* are set in italic type when they appear with the chemical name or formula and are never capitalized.

Accents

Marks placed over, under, or through a character as a guide to pronunciation. In non-English languages, accents represent certain sounds. Typeset accents used to be separate characters and did not exist as one unit. The letter had to be combined with the accent in order to create the accented letter. Today, with page-layout and word-processing programs, most accented characters are created by placing the proper accent—which has zero width—below, above, or through the character.

Accent	PC	Mac	
Acute	´	Shift-option-E	″
Angstrom	Not available	Option-K	å
Macron	‾	Shift-option-,	$
Cedilla	‚	Shift-option-Z	ç
Circumflex	˄	Shift-option-I	ê
Diaeresis	¨	Shift-option-U	ö
Grave	`	`	à
Breve	Not available	Shift-option-.	ˇ
Tilde	~	Shift-option-N	ñ
Umlaut	¨	Shift-option-U	ï
(also called Diaeresis)			
Caron	Not available	Shift-option-T	a
Overdot	Not available	Option-H	·

The use of a separate accent that floats over the characters is called, naturally enough, a floating accent. To accomplish this, font systems must keep track of all character widths, and the lowly lowercase i must not have a dot—it also floats, even for normal use.

Following are some accents used in languages that have English alphabetic characters:

Danish	ÅØåéøÆæ
Finnish	ÄÅäåö
German	ÅÖÜåöü
French	ÀÂÇÉÈÊËÎÏÔÙÛÜàâçéèêëîïôùûüŒœ
Hungarian	ÁÉÍÓÖÚÜáéíóöúü
Icelandic	ÁÉÍÓÖ°Úáðéíó˛ú″
Italian	ÀÈÌÎÒÙàèìîòù
Spanish	ÁÉÍÑÓÚÜáéíñóúü

Quotes

Quotation marks were originally commas, and in the 1600s looked like the present French quotes (« »). English printers refused to use the French form and inverted the comma at the beginning of quoted material and used apostrophes at the close. In French and Spanish, small angle marks on the lower part of the type body are used for quotations. In German, two primes are used.

Opening and closing punctuation marks indicate verbal statements or emphasize certain words. Double quotes are normally used, and single quotes are used within a double quotation. Quotation marks were originally commas placed in the outer margins, and were applied by Morel of Paris in 1557. For good display typography, use quotes one size smaller than the text.

Most people who do not have any typographic skills do not know the difference between quotes and prime marks. One identifier of a good typographer is the use of curly quotes in typographic work. Curly quotes or "smart quotes" can be turned on in some applications so that they will look like the following:

"Michelle was 8'11" tall and could dunk a basketball like no one else."

Proper use of quotes and prime marks.

Prime marks and quotation marks are not the same thing. A single prime mark is used to show feet or minutes, and a double prime mark is used to show inches or seconds. The prime marks usually are found in the symbol fonts, and can be used by selecting the symbol font or pressing the following key commands:

Character	Mac	PC
´	Option-4	Alt-0162
´´	Option-comma	Alt-0178
'	Command-'	Control-'
''	Command-shift-'	Control-alt-'

When creating a file that will be used on both the Macintosh and PC, it is necessary to choose a font that is available to both platforms. A common problem is choosing a prime mark from a font that is not available for the Macintosh. When an unavailable symbol font is chosen, the Macintosh will substitute a character for the prime mark.

Single quotes are used for quoted material within a double quotation, although in Great Britain this practice is reversed. In some cases a space is needed to separate the quote from the first letter.

Quotes that are longer than five sentences long should be separated from the rest of the text with an indent on one side or both sides, as an extract. This may be set in a slightly smaller type size or in italic. The following rules apply when doing this:

- The quoted material should be one size smaller than the body text.
- Leading should be no more than 2 extra points greater than the quoted type size.
- Indent 2 picas maximum from left and right margins.
- Quotation marks are not needed when material is indented. Setting the quote off from the body text eliminates the need for them.
- Paragraph indents in quoted matter should be indented an additional em space.

- Significant omissions in a long quote can be shown by asterisks instead of ellipses. Assign 4 to 6 points of leading before the next line of copy when doing this. The asterisks should also be centered and on their own line; never should they appear on the same line as text.
- Punctuation at the end of a quotation always goes outside the quotation. If there are single and double quotes together, the punctuation is placed either within the single quote followed by the double quote or between them, depending on the sense.

Grace said, "Then Tom told me, 'Go west, young man, and make sure you do not fall into the canyon.'"

Grace asked, "Did you hear him say, "Go west, young man'?"

Dashes
There are a few types of dashes used in typography. Primary ones:
Hyphen (-)   En dash (–)   Em dash (—)

Hyphen
Hyphens break words on syllables at the end of lines to allow even spacing in justification and for compound or connected words. Hyphens are used to connect words, phrases, etc. One of the first signs of typographic experience is the proper use of hyphens. When determining whether a hyphen should be used or not, the following rules must be followed:

I shook the two-sided die four times and ended up with a six.

- Always use a hyphen when breaking a word at the end of a line.
- Always use a hyphen when connecting two or more words to create a compound phrase.
- Never use any spaces before a hyphen.
- Use spaces after a hyphen only in multiple-modifying cases, such as "thirty- and fifty-year-olds."

Some people separate the word pre-press with a hyphen.

En dash
En dashes are used where the words *to* or *through* are represented, such as "pages 1–9" or January 13–19." The en dash also connects two nouns of equal weight, as in "east–west." It may also replace a colon.

If no en dash exists, kern two hyphens together. Spacing around the en dash should be closed, so that there is no spacing on either side. The en dash is one-half the width of the em dash and is longer than a hyphen.

En—equal to half of a typeface's point size, half the width of an em.

| PC: | control + alt + shift + hyphen |
| Mac: | option + hyphen |

Three-quarter em dash
The ¾ em dash is slightly smaller than a regular em dash, and is used where the em dash would appear too wide for the typeface. Not all fonts have a ¾ em dash.

Em dash
Em dashes indicate missing material or are used for parenthetical remarks or to show a break and add special emphasis. Em dashes can sometimes replace colons.

Em dashes may be set *open*, with a space on either side, or *closed*, with no space. Pick one approach and stick with it.

| Open — open | Space on both sides |
| Closed—closed | No space on either side |

An em is the square of the point size:

Em width

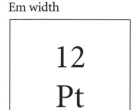

12
Pt

En width

6
Pt

PC: control + alt + shift + =
Mac: command + option + spacebar

Figures
Figures refer to numerals. In most style conventions, arabic numerals under 10 are spelled out, unless they relate to references or specific measurements. In almost all cases, spell out numerals at the beginning of a sentence. Figures should be the same width to allow them to line up in tables or lists; this does not apply to dates. Watch old habits of typing; the letter O and number 0 as well as the letter l and numeral 1 are very different.

1 1	1 1	1 1	1 1
O 0	O 0	O0	O 0
Times	Courier	Minion	Garamond

You should spell out a number that appear at the beginning of a sentence. Also, some prefer all numbers under 100, like twenty, to be spelled out, as well as large whole numbers such as one thousand. Numbers should also be spelled out if they are not used often, even if the number is large.

> The mailman dropped off four hundred packages before heading back to the post office, being chased by fifty-five attack dogs.

There should be uniform style throughout a document. If numbers are spelled out in one chapter, they should also be done that way in all the following chapters. Words are preferred to numbers, generally, and should always be used in legal documents. Dollar amounts should always be expressed in numerals unless they are a part of a legal contract. Common sense should dictate the use of figures in all documents.

Old style (nonaligning)

1 2 3 4 5 6 7 8 9 0

Old-style figures are a style of numeric figures used with old-style roman typefaces. If not available in a particular font, old-style figures can be created by using the lowercase or small-cap "I" for the numeral "1" and the lowercase "O" for "0." By juggling the rest of the numerals up or down, they will look like old-style numerals. These figures are nonaligning figures, since the ascenders and descenders do not line up. Some of the descenders fall below the baseline, just like the lowercase letters do in some fonts. In most cases, old-style numbers are appropriate and will help to enhance the typographic look of a page.

Lining (modern)

1 2 3 4 5 6 7 8 9 0

Lining figures are a style of numeric figures used with most type-faces. Lining numerals are the same height as caps when used with upper and lowercase, though they tend to stick out just a little too much.

Lining numerals should be used when mixing numbers with all-uppercase text. If old-style numbers are not available, it sometimes may enhance the appearance to decrease the point size of the lining numerals so they do not stick out as much. Lining figures work best in tabular material.

Rich was born on August 30, 1967.

Rob was born on July 14, 1972.

Roman
Roman numerals are considered the formal system of figures and are only used in special instances. The chart below gives examples of some roman numerals.

1	I	30	XXX	200	CC
2	II	40	XL	400	CD
4	IV	41	XLI	500	D
5	V	49	IL	600	DC
6	VI	50	L	900	CM
7	VII	60	LX	1000	M
9	IX	90	XC	1981	MCMLXXXI
10	X	100	C	2000	MM
11	XI	101	CI	5000	V̄
20	XX	150	CL	10,000	X̄

Let's see you put these into an Excel spreadsheet:

Polonious   *LXII*
Claudius   *LXXIV*
Caesar   *MCM*

Em fractions
This is the most common form of fraction, with each fraction on the em width, with a diagonal stroke. Most expert sets have at least the 1/4, 1/2, and 3/4 characters. You can create fractions very easily with the fraction bar set to the whole number's point size, and the numerator and whole number aligning at the baseline.

In a proper fraction, the numerator and denominator are usually 60 percent of the whole number's point size and 90 percent of its width. More importantly, the numbers are kerned to the stroke, between −11 and −22 units.

$\frac{7}{8}$

This is what they are supposed to look like:

$\frac{1}{8}$ $\frac{5}{8}$ $\frac{7}{8}$ $\frac{1}{3}$ $\frac{2}{3}$ $\frac{1}{2}$ $\frac{1}{4}$ $\frac{3}{4}$

Manufactured fractions are created by selecting the numerator and changing it to a superscript and changing the denominator to a subscript, but you may also need to make them even smaller and then shift the baseline to get them properly positioned. You should use a solidus, found in the expert fonts, instead of a regular slash. A regular slash is not set at the correct angle to look right.

En fraction
En fractions are on the en width, with a horizontal stroke. They are also called case or stacked fractions. These are used with the wide variety of odd fractions, as one might find in a plumbing catalog. However, metric measurements are replacing weird inch fractions.

$\dfrac{7}{8}$

To create this fraction, place the denominator on one line and hit the return key. Place the denominator right under the numerator on the line below. Select the denominator and press command-shift-N on the Macintosh or control-shift-N on the PC.

The following dialog box will appear on the screen:

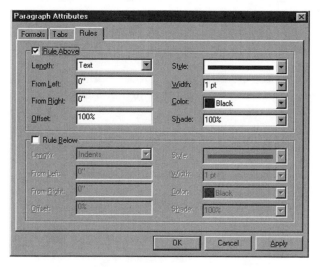

Rule dialog box in QuarkXPress for the PC.

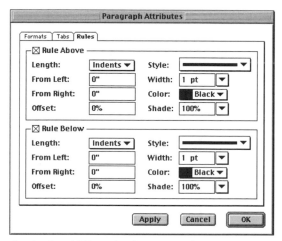

Rule dialog box in QuarkXPress for the Macintosh.

The length should be set to Text, not Indents, so the rule is only as long as the fraction. The rule should be no wider than 1 point, or it will look out of place. By highlighting the denominator, Rule Above is clicked; if the numerator is highlighted, Rule Below is selected.

Piece fractions
Piece fractions are created using en and em versions of characters with only denominators. Fractions are created using special numerals, such as superiors, in combination with the denominator to form the full fraction.

Numerators are "created" using special numerators, such as the superiors, which position with the denominator to form the full fraction.

$$^1+ /8 = \tfrac{1}{8}$$

Fake fractions
Normal-size numerators separated by a slash. The hyphen should be used to make 1 1/4 look like 1-1/4. This style should only be used if there is no alternative available.

Expert set fractions
⅛ ⅝ ⅞ ⅓ ⅔ ½ ¼ ¾

Decimal fractions
2.33

Spell out fractions
Two and one-third

Make sure that the fraction matches the typeface.

The slash that should be used for fractions is not the same slash that is located on the keyboard. For the Macintosh, the fraction bar, or solidus, can be created in most fonts by pressing option-shift-1. For the PC format, expert sets are necessary to create the solidus.

7/8   ⅞

As can be seen in this example, the fraction bar is properly used on the right and is at more of an angle than the keyboard slash on the left.

Ligatures

Ligatures are two or more characters designed as a single unit. Gutenberg's font had many ligatures (more than 150) in order to simulate handwriting and to achieve even word spacing in his justified columns. Most ligatures have to do with the f, since it takes up the most horizontal space of any letter. In foundry type, the f actually extended beyond its metal body. Without the ligature, the typographer would have to cut off the dot of the letter i to make room for the overlap of the f. Some typefaces are designed not to need ligatures. Our example below uses Minion, which has the problem, but Palatino, shown at the bottom of the page, does not.

The majority of sans-serif typefaces do not use ligatures, an example being Optima. There are five f-ligatures plus the diphthongs: ff, fi, fl, ffi, and ffl. On the Macintosh, the ligatures fi and fl are a part of the regular character font sets. These can be created by pressing option-shift-5 and option-shift-6, respectively. In Windows, creating the ligatures takes a little bit more work, since there are no shortcut keys to create them. The easiest way to get a ligature is to open an expert font in the character map and copy the ligature into the document, or check to see what the keyboard command is. Ligatures usually are used only in text sizes, though in special cases they are used in display sizes.

Another place where ligatures should never be used is in type that has been expanded or condensed. Since these characters are spread out, the ligature will stick out like a sore thumb, since the ligatures contain the only characters touching one another. Book production usually uses them, though magazines do not. In the Gutenberg font, there are a wide number of ligatures that were available.

If Joanna kindly omitted various entities, now the fish could flip and flop from the floor back into the river.

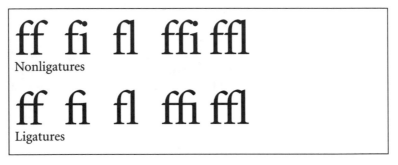

ff fi fl ffi ffl
Nonligatures

ff fi fl ffi ffl
Ligatures

It is possible to do a search and replace throughout an entire document. In the search window, the ligature may not display properly, though it will work correctly. Just make sure that the correct characters are placed in the dialog box.

Be careful when using ligatures since they create a tight letter combination that may appear in a word with loosely spaced letters.

Diphthongs
Also considered ligatures are ß, œ, Œ, æ, and Æ. They were created from the need to indicate a particular sound and usually consist of two vowels. These are also sometimes called non-English ligatures. The multiple characters that comprise a diphthong are almost always pronounced as one letter, unlike a ligature, where both letters are pronounced individually.

fs   oe   CE   ae   AE
Nonligatures

ß   œ   Œ   æ   Æ
Ligatures

Ampersand

The ampersand was originally a ligature and was Latin for the word "and." In Latin, it was *et per se*, and eventually was passed on through time and ended up being *and per se*. Eventually it finally became the word ampersand.

One of the first examples of an ampersand appears on a piece of papyrus from about 45 A.D. Written in the style of early Roman capital cursive, it shows the ligature ET. A sample of Pompeian graffiti from 79 A.D. also shows a combination of the capitals E and T, and is again written in early Roman script. Later documents display a more flowing lowercase cursive, which evolved into our italic, and the appearance of a ligature et becomes more frequent. While the connection between the capital letters E and T was initially formed by writing quickly, later calligraphic manuscripts show the middle part of the E, consisting of semicircles, joined to the T by an intentional horizontal line.

Eventually, this combination began to look like one symbol. By the time scribes developed Carolingian minuscule about 775 A.D., the ligature had become a standard part of their repertoire. Depending on the writing speed or the calligrapher's concern for perfection, from the eighth century on, the combination of the letters E and T resembled the ligature that was adopted with the invention of printing in the early 15th century.

The left-hand portion of the ampersand is either a lowercase e or a capital E consisting of two semicircles. The oblique upstroke, often with a drop-shaped terminal, might be a leftover from the horizontal stroke in E or e, or it might have been one of the lines connecting to the next character, a technique preferred by calligraphers to increase the flow of writing. Compared to the italic form, the roman version of the ampersand in general shows only a meager remainder of the t-stroke.

Today, the ampersand is incorporated into the design of every new font and is a part of every existing roman alphabet. The variations of the ampersand vary to great degrees, particularly in italics. With the appearance of slab-serif and sans-serif typefaces in the nineteenth century, type founders preferred the roman version of the ampersand (&) in italic as well as roman styles.

Ampersand usage varies from language to language. In English and French text, the ampersand may be substituted for the words "and" and "et," and both versions may be used in the same text. The German rule is to use the ampersand within formal or corporate titles made up of two separate names; according to present German composition rules, the ampersand may not be used in running text.

In any language, the ampersand's calligraphic qualities make it a compelling design element that can add visual appeal and personality to any page.

Setting an ampersand in small caps sometimes works better than the usng the standard cap version. In some styles, it is also possible to see the letters e and t incorporated into the character itself. Though ampersands should be used in titles and company names, it is generally not appropriate for running text. Sometimes making an ampersand italic makes it fit in better with the rest of the text.

Caps & lowercase (cap &)
Caps & lowercase (small-cap &)

Ballot boxes

Boxes should be as close to the x-height as possible if used full size, and centered on the x-height if they're set smaller. Usually, ballot boxes should be set smaller so they do not stick out. Most often you will have to change the point size of boxes so they match the x-height. They usually possess a drop shadow and are used in bulleted lists. Ballot boxes may also be circles.

The purpose of ballot boxes is to give emphasis to text segments or words. In magazines, ballot boxes are sometimes used to signal the end of a story. When this is done, it is placed after a word space right after the last word in the story.

Most often they are used in coupons or forms to be checked. There is no open ballot box in the PostScript font. Choose Zapf Dingbats, type lowercase n, the solid box, and then make it an outline.

Open   Closed

☐ This box tends to stick out.
▫ This box does not, and fits in better with the text, but is a little too small.

Bullets

Bulleted lists are used quite often in books, magazines, and other forms of writing. To create a bullet on the Macintosh, the command is option-8. On the PC, a bullet is created by pressing alt-0149. Why not consider trying other characters as bullets? There are so many symbols in the symbol fonts that one of them may look better.

Interesting characters that could be used for bullets include some of the following:

Rules

The rule line is used for horizontal ruling to indicate underlining. A rule is an em-width dash, repeated to form a line. Not all dashes can form a solid line when repeated. For underscoring you want the baseline rule, which aligns at the baseline of the font.

The problem with a typographically created line of rules is that the width of the rule may not divide evenly into the line length. Rules are commonly of em width, the width of the point size. If the line length is an even number of picas, the 12-point rule would divide evenly. If the line length is in half-picas, then a 6-point rule would divide evenly.

The lightest weight rule is called a hairline rule. Be careful about using it. It outputs a set of spots at the resolution of the printer. This is fine at 600 DPI (1/600th of an inch), but at 2,400 DPI the rule disappears.

Rule widths are in increments of a point, but you can use fractions of a point. We suggest you use .25, .33, or .5 points.

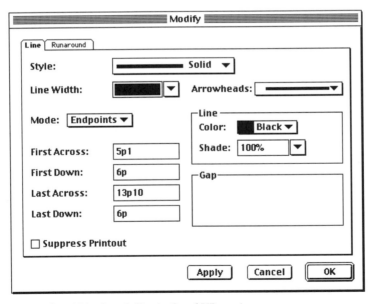

Setting the width of a rule line in QuarkXPress 4.

Hairline rule

Half-point rule

One-point rule

Two-point rule

Four-point rule

Six-point rule

Eight-point rule

Twelve-point rule

One-point coupon rule

Two-point coupon rule

One-point right arrow rule, no tail

One-point left arrow rule, no tail

One-point right arrow rule, with tail

One-point left arrow rule, with tail

One-point double-headed arrow rule

The half-point rule is the thinnest rule that is commonly used. Only when printing offset on quality paper should the hairline be used. In newspaper printing, hairlines are difficult to see, because of the porous paper and production process. Hairlines in a reverse or on a nonwhite background tend to fill in and disappear.

When using rules to go around a box, make sure they do not overpower the text or picture inside the box. Ornamental dashes (rules) are used primarily to separate elements, to signal the end of an informational segment. Rules combine best with traditional roman or blackletter typefaces.

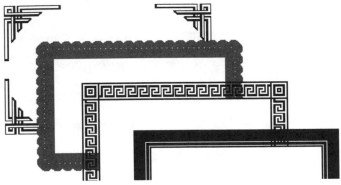

Ornamental borders.

Ellipsis

Ellipsis dots indicate that something is missing, or conversation has stopped. They show that the author is purposely leaving out a word or words in quoted material, and may also express a pause in thought. At the end of a complete sentence, use four dots, one being the period. Digital type fonts provide ellipses as one character sometimes, to save time for the user. A single space should always be left before and after the ellipsis, except when another punctuation mark is used. Be sure to use fixed spaces within the points of ellipsis; problems can occur if the ellipsis breaks at the end of a line.

. . .	Spaced with word spaces
. . .	Spaced with en spaces
. . .	Spaced using punctuation spaces
...	Created using alt-0133 on the PC

The last two versions look best, and the spaces should be about half the size of the en space. Some problems may occur if ellipses are not created correctly:

- If spaced with thin spaces, the typesetting equipment may see surrounding words as one unit and break them, thus forcing a tight line or a badly spaced one.
- If using word spaces, you might have erratic spacing—too wide or too close—based on the justification of the line, though the word space will help if the dots fall at the end of the line. An alternative is kerned word spaces.
- You can separate the dots with thin spaces and insert a kerned word space between them and the preceding word.
- Use kerned word spaces between the periods.

Footnotes and references
Footnotes are marginal, parenthetical, or reference material related to the main text, positioned at the bottom of the page and called out by symbols, letters, or numbers. Usually these callouts appear as superiors. A footnote must fall on the same page as its reference mark but may be carried over to the bottom of successive pages. A short rule or added space should separate the text from the footnote. The first line can be indented or flush left and may be placed at the end of the text that it refers to.

Footnotes are usually set in 7- or 8-point type. By law, footnotes in financial forms, annual reports, and other SEC documents must be no smaller than the text size, which is 10 point. The sequence for the symbols that call out footnotes is:

Order	Example
1. Asterisk	*
2. Dagger	†
3. Double dagger	‡
4. Paragraph symbol	¶
5. Section mark	§
6. Parallel rules	‖
7. Number sign	#

Footnote/reference marks in the order they should be used.

If more are needed, then the marks should be doubled up. For example: double asterisk, double single dagger, double double dagger, double paragraph symbol, etc. When material has a large number of references, it may be easier to use consecutive numbers instead of the footnote symbols. When numerals are used, the footnote number should always follow the punctuation mark in text, unless it is a dash, and set at the end of the sentence. If the numbers are set between a subject and a verb or between other related words, it will become distracting to the reader. Proper placement would look like this:

"I do not know," said Elana.[5]

Proper use of a numerical reference mark.

Drop caps

To make a piece of typographic work look more elegant, drop caps can be added. Drop caps were originally used to create a professional look to a document, as well as to signal the start of a chapter or segment, and were done by hand. Today's drop caps are not as fancy or as large as they used to be, though they serve the same purpose.

A drop cap is sometimes also known as a sunken initial. This version has an initial letter set so that the top of the initial is even with the top of the first line of type. The initial is made larger than the rest of the text but is the first letter of the paragraph.

Two letters that usually do not work well with this type of drop cap are the A and L, since the excess space between the letter and the text is not visually pleasing. With the letters I and T, the space is so small that it causes the same problem. We prefer at least one line of type after the lines of the drop cap to "frame" the big letter in a way.

Another type of drop cap is a raised initial, in which the initial rests on the baseline of the first line of text and rises above the first line of text. With raised initials, more white space is required, which is why newspapers usually stick to the sunken initial.

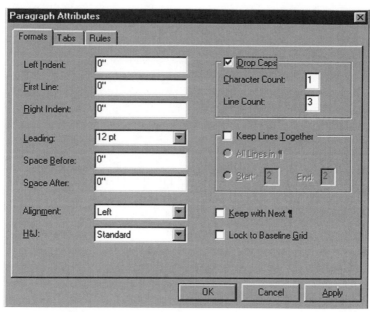

The Paragraph Attributes dialog box, where drop caps can be created in the PC version of QuarkXPress.

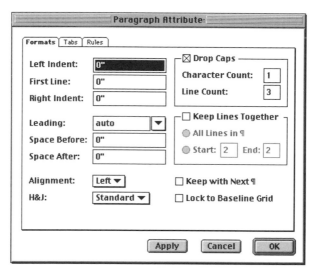

The Paragraph Attributes box, where drop caps can be created in the Macintosh version of QuarkXPress.

The space around the initial should be the same on the right side and the bottom of the letter. A raised initial should always be on the baseline, though, and kerning should be applied as necessary.

Traditionally, the first word following the initial should be set in small caps. The lines adjacent to the cap should be contoured to flow around the curves or strokes of the letter to enhance the appearance.

This is an example of what a raised initial would look like. Notice how the letter lines up with the baseline of the first line of text and raises above the ascender line. The first word is in all lowercase.

THIS is an example of what a raised initial would look like. Notice how the letter lines up with the baseline of the first line of text and raises above the ascender line. The first word is in all uppercase.

THIS is an example of what a raised initial would look like. Notice how the letter lines up with the baseline of the first line of text and raises above the ascender line. The first word is in small caps.

This is an example of what a sunken initial would look like. Notice how the letter lines up with the ascenders of the first line of text and falls below the descender line. The first word is in all lowercase.

THIS is an example of what a sunken initial would look like. Notice how the letter lines up with the ascenders of the first line of text and falls below the descender line. The first word is in all uppercase.

THIS is an example of what a sunken initial would look like. Notice how the letter lines up with the ascenders of the first line of text and falls below the descender line. The first word is in small caps.

Small caps

abx GHI ghi CDR

Most of the characters we read are at the x-height.

Small caps match the x-height of a particular type and size and are slightly expanded. There are two types of small caps: *manufactured* and *true*. Manufactured small caps can be created by some software programs. In QuarkXPress when you tell the program to use small caps, it is not a true form but created by reducing the font size, and may also not be the same weight.

THESE ARE MANUFACTURED SMALL CAPS BY QUARKXPRESS.

THESE ARE ACTUAL SMALL CAPS DESIGNED BY THE TYPE DESIGNER.

Manufactured and actual small caps.

True small caps are the same as the x-height and are usually equal to the normal cap width. Some programs create their own, but true small caps are only found in expert typefaces. Depending on the typeface, additional letterspacing may need to be added if the characters look too crowded or tight. Text that is all caps should be done in small caps, as well as abbreviations of awards, decorations, honors, titles, etc. following a person's name.

In the old days they were used for awards, decorations, honors, titles, etc., following a person's name. Words that are specified as all caps may look better in small caps. Old-style figures also look best with small caps.

February 12, 1954
FEBRUARY 12, 1954

Use all caps or small caps for the following:
- For the word WHEREAS.
- For the word NOTE introducing an explanatory paragraph that cannot be used as a footnote.
- For the words SECTION and ARTICLE in reference to part of a document by number.
- For the speaker in a dialogue or play.
- For ascription to author of a direct, independent quotation.
- For words ordinarily in italics that appear in an all-cap-and-small-cap or in an all-small-cap line.
- For the abbreviations A.M. and P.M. and B.C. and A.D. There should be no space between the letters.

Small capitals are useful for section headings or chapter titles, to accent important words or phrases in midsentence, or at the beginning of a paragraph for a lead-in. True small caps are one sign of a truly professional job.

Swash

ABCDEFGHIJKLMONOPQRSTUVWXYZ

Swash characters are uppercase letters that have flourishes added to them. Originally they were designed to go with italic typefaces and can be found in the expert sets of fonts.

Swash caps should be used sparingly. Here are a few bad examples:

RON

HAPPY HOLIDAYS

Welcome to *RIT*

Logotypes

When each piece of type was set separately, the words had to be assembled individually into lines. Common combinations were often made into single units to save time. These single units were called logotypes. Eventually combinations of letters and special characters were used to express a product or idea.

The name was then used for any image that was prepared and repeated, such as trade names. A logo is a specifically designed company name—often with a symbol—that emphasizes typography. Today, logotypes represent companies or products.

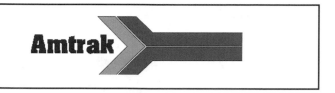

Examples of logotypes.

Expert sets

Expert sets are fonts containing a set of accents with their vowels, small caps, fractions, and other specialty characters, in addition to the basic set of characters. Using an expert set allows the user to be more creative in setting type. Chances are you would never use an expert set without also using the regular font. For example, if using Garamond Expert, in most cases you will be mixing it with the font Garamond to make sure it looks correct.

In the font Minion Expert, the following characters are found in the expert set:

ABCDEFGHIJKLMNOPQRSTUVWX
1234567890 Đ ¾⅝⅞⅓⅔
ffflffiffl₡Rp:
143^{b}6¨¢9Ł7^{9156}¿ r a
ÀÁÂÃÄÅÆÇÈÉÊËÌÍÎÏ$
ÑÒÓÔÕÖ¡ØÙÚÛÜŸ

All the characters found in the typeface Minion Expert.

In setting stock quotes, the expert set may be very helpful, as well enhance the look of the document. For example:

Stock	*Close*	*Open*
Carroll & Co.	12-5/8	– 1/8
Ricard & Co.	37 ⅝	– ⅛

In tabular and financial information, fractions in the expert fonts may help to enhance the presentation.

4

Digital Typography

Pica was originally a type size, roughly equal to a 12-point setting. Today, it is the basic measurement of type. There are 6 picas in an inch.

Europe uses the Didot system, in which:

> 1 corps = .01483"
> 12 corps = 1 cicero (.178")

Mediaan system
This system, used primarily in Belgium, uses a corps measuring system of .01374 inch. The Mediaan em, or cicero, measures .165 inch. Now the Didot (point) system is mostly used.

In the desktop environment:

> 1 point = .01388"
> 12 points = 1 pica (.166")
> 72 points = 1 inch

Points	American	Didot	Mediaan
1	.01383	.01483	.01374
2	.0277	.0296	.0275
4	.0553	.0593	.0550
4.25	.0657	.0704	.0653
5	.0692	.0742	.0687
5.5	.0761	.0816	.0756
6	.0830	.0890	.0824
6.25	.0899	.0964	.0893
6.5	.0934	.1001	.0927
7	.0968	.1038	.0962
7.5	.1037	.1112	.1031
7.25	.1072	.1149	.1065
8	.1107	.1186	.1099
8.5	.1176	.1261	.1168
9	.1245	.1335	.1237
10	.1383	.1483	.1374
10.5	.1452	.1557	.1443
11	.1522	.1631	.1511
11.5	.1591	.1705	.1580
12	.1660	.1780	.1649
14	.1936	.2076	.1924
16	.2213	.2373	.2198
18	.2490	.2669	.2473
20	.2767	.2966	.2748
21	.2906	.3114	.2885
24	.3320	.3559	.3298
27	.3736	.4004	.3710
28	.3874	.4152	.3847
30	.4150	.4449	.4122
34	.4704	.5042	.4672
36	.4980	.5339	.4946

To convert from one system to another, use the following:

mm x 2.8453	To get points
mm x .2371	To get picas
mm x .0394	To get inches
Points x .3515	To get mm
Points x .08335	To get picas
Points x .0138	To get inches
Picas x 4.2175	To get mm
Picas x 12.0	To get points
Picas x .166	To get inches
Inches x 25.4	To get mm
Inches x 72.27	To get picas
Inches x 6.0225	To get picas

Point size is more than the vertical distance of the overall typeface design, from top of tallest character to the bottom of the longest character. It is a fixed number, and a face may use all or some of that space. Much of Europe is moving to purely metric measurements. Because some faces have very long ascenders and descenders, these typefaces look smaller than others with short ascenders and descenders when both are printed at the same point size.

Spacing
Spacing is the amount of unused space that exists between words, letters, and lines. Spacing provides a means to avoid overlapping shapes and letters to improve readability as well as legibility. A basic rule of spacing is that if you notice the spacing, there is too much. Common types of fixed spaces are the em, en, and thin spaces. The en space is one-half of the em space, and the thin space is either one-quarter or one-third of the em. The em is the square of the point size, so it has no value unless the point size is defined.

Em space:	Use two ens

| Indented one em (two ens)
| Indented two ems (four ens)
| Indented three ems (six ens)
| Indented four ems (eight ens)

En space: PC: control + shift + 6
                Mac: option + space

| Indented one en
| Indented two ens
| Indented three ens

Flexible space: PC: control + alt + shift + 5
                 Mac: command + option + space

| Indented one flexible space
| Indented two flexible spaces
| Indented three flexible spaces
| Indented four flexible spaces

Optical spacing

It is difficult to have consistent spacing in typography because of optical illusions caused by the shapes of characters and the proximity of letter shapes. Letters are made of three basic shapes:

Oval   *Inclined*   *Vertical*

The combined appearance of the spacing between letters is called optical volume. Characters have some basic characteristics that they share with other characters. For example, the letters f, i, j, r, t, and l all are made up of narrow, upright strokes. Today, the kerning options usually take care of the optical volume problems, which is very important for display type—defined as type larger than 14 point.

In this optical illusion, the spaces between the squares and circles look different, even though they are the same.

In this example, the space between the circles was decreased, to make it seem that the space is equal between the squares and circles.

In other words, for spacing to look even and consistent in typography, it must be inconsistent. Optical spacing cannot be achieved by numbers alone. You must use your eye and develop a sense of what is acceptable or not.

Horizontal spacing
When spacing along a line, use the tab key or even a fixed space. Do not use the spacebar to try to position characters on a line.

Letterspacing
Letterspacing is the addition or subtraction of space between letters. Word space values are also usually adjusted. Letterspacing is best used to modify headings and should be applied with caution in text, since too much spacing makes copy difficult to read.

Some programs automatically add letterspacing when the text is justified. This directly affects readability by controlling word shapes. Text that is all caps or placed in small caps may seem too tight and may need additional letterspace added to it.

	Track set to
ABCabcdefGHIjklMNOpqrSTUvwxyz	−5
ABCabcdefGHIjklMNOpqrSTUvwxyz	−4
ABCabcdefGHIjklMNOpqrSTUvwxyz	−3
ABCabcdefGHIjklMNOpqrSTUvwxyz	−2
ABCabcdefGHIjklMNOpqrSTUvwxyz	−1
ABCabcdefGHIjklMNOpqrSTUvwxyz	0
ABCabcdefGHIjklMNOpqrSTUvwxyz	+1
ABCabcdefGHIjklMNOpqrSTUvwxyz	+2
ABCabcdefGHIjklMNOpqrSTUvwxyz	+3
ABCabcdefGHIjklMNOpqrSTUvwxyz	+4
ABCabcdefGHIjklMNOpqrSTUvwxyz	+5

Kerning

Kerning is the selective addition or subtraction of space between letters and between words. In QuarkXPress, a kerning unit is equal to 1/300th of an em. In newer programs, it is even finer than that. This function can cause characters to overlap if too much space is subtracted. It is used as an optical adjustment function to make larger type look better visually. Below are some examples of kerned letters:

Washington	No kerning
Washington	−10 for all
Washington	Different values for each letter combination
Washington	No kerning

Examining optical and fixed kerning in QuarkXPress.

In the preceding example, lines one and four are typed with no adjustments. Line two was done with fixed kerning, by changing the tracking to –10. The third line was done with optical kerning, by changing the amount between each letter to make it look good.

In line three, the value between the W and a is –20, while the value between the letters a and s is –5.

Visually we move one character into the preceding character's block. Kerning can be done in QuarkXPress by using the measurement palette or under the Style menu. Under the Style menu, tracking is changed by highlighting the characters to be kerned and choosing a percentage of track.

This can be applied to two letters or to a whole word at once. When doing a whole word, do not select the last letter, or the space between words will also increase or decrease.

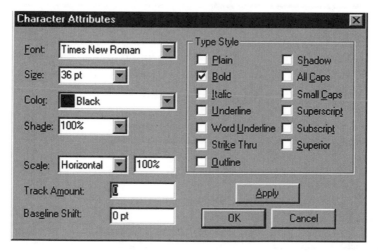

Screen shot of a PC dialog box for kerning and tracking.

Screen shot of the measurements palette in QuarkXPress.

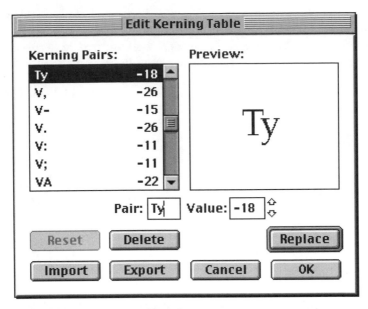

QuarkXPress Macintosh kern table dialog.

Automatic kerning can only work if the font manufacturer has built the capability into its fonts. You can add to the set, but be aware that additional sets of kern pairs take up computer memory and system resources.

You can kern or track individual character pairs, words, or lines from the measurements palette in QuarkXPress by entering an amount in the area shown below where the "–4" is located.

Another option is to use the keyboard shortcut keys, which are shown on the next page.

	Macintosh
− .005 em	command-option-shift-[
+ .005 em	command-option-shift-]
− .05 em	command-shift-[
+ .05 em	command-shift-]
	Windows
− .005 em	control-alt-shift-[
+ .005 em	control-alt-shift-]
− .05 em	control-shift-[
+ .05 em	control-shift-]

QuarkXPress keyboard commands for kerning.

Automatic kerning in some applications is the default, which may not be acceptable to the designer. Some programs can hold up to 200 character pairs that can be predetermined. Kerning can solve the following:

- Parts of a letter are extending beyond the body of type.
- Adjusting space between characters. Selectively used between pairs of letters. Some programs contain kerning tables. Computers can now be set to remember kerning pairs and kern automatically. Kerning will therefore be consistent throughout the document.

To add or adjust kerning pairs in QuarkXPress, click on Kerning Table Edit under the Utilities menu. The dialog box that appears will display all the fonts in which you can adjust kerning pairs.

Since every font is a little different, a pair that needs kerning in one font may not need to be adjusted in another font. Select the font and and click Edit. The following screen then appears:

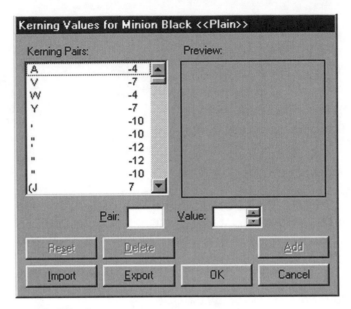

Kerning edit dialog box.

By placing two character in the pair box, and then choosing a value, pairs of characters can be automatically kerned in a font. The preview box shows what the characters look like with the kerning value chosen, so the correct amount can be set. Once the additional characters have been added, click OK, and they will be always be kerned when that typeface is used.

The top twenty kerning pairs that are most annoying and should be corrected when typesetting:

Yo, We, To, Tr, Ta, Wo, Tu, Tw, Ya, Te, P., Ty, Wa, yo, we, T., Y., TA, PA, WA

The above may be the top twenty pairs, but there is an extended list on the next few pages:

AC	AT	AV	AW	AY	FA	LT	LV
LW	LY	OA	OV	OW	OY	PA	TA
TO	VA	VO	WA	WO	YA	YO	Av
Aw	Ay	A'	A-	A–	F.	F,	F-
F–	L'	L-	L–	P.	P,	P;	P:
P-	R-	R–	Ta	Te	Ti	To	Tu
Tw	Ty	T.	T,	T;	T-	T–	Va
Ve	Vi	Vo	Vu	V.	V,	V;	V:
V-	V–	Wa	We	Wi	Wo	Wr	Wu
Wy	W.	W,	W;	W:	W-	W–	Ya
Ye	Yi	Yo	Yu	Y.	Y;	Y:	Y-
Y–	ff	fi	fl	rm	rn	rt	ry
r.	r,	r-	r–	y.	y,	'S	's
AG	AO	AQ	AU	BA	BE	BL	BP
BR	BU	BV	BW	BY	CA	CO	CR
DA	DD	DR	DI	DL	DM	DN	DO
DP	DR	DU	DV	DW	DY	EC	EO
FC	FG	FO	GE	GO	GR	GU	HO
IC	IG	IO	JA	JO	KO	LC	LG
LO	LU	MC	MG	MO	NC	NG	NO
OB	OD	OE	OF	OH	OI	OK	OL
OM	ON	OP	OR	OT	OU	OX	PE
PL	PO	PP	PU	PY	QU	RC	RG

RO	RT	RU	RV	RW	RY	SI	SM
ST	SU	TC	C.	C,	Da	D.	D,
Eu	Fa	Fe	Fi	Fo	Fr	Ft	Fu
Fy	F;	F:	Gu	He	Ho	Hu	Hy
Ic	Id	Iq	Io	It	Ja	Je	Jo
Ju	J.	J,	Ke	Ko	Ku	K-	K–
Lu	LY	Ma	Mc	Md	Me	Mo	Mu
Na	Ne	Ni	No	Nu	N.	N,	Oa
Ob	Oh	Ok	Ol	O.	O,	Pa	Pe
Po	Rd	Re	Ro	Rt	Ru	Si	Sp
Su	S.	S,	Ua	Ug	Um	Un	Up
Us	U.	U,	Wd	Wm	Wt	Yd	ac
ad	ae	ag	ap	af	at	au	av
aw	ay	ap	bl	br	bu	by	b.
b,	ca	ch	ck	da	dc	de	dg
do	dt	du	dv	dw	dy	d.	d,
ea	ei	el	em	en	ep	er	et
eu	ev	ew	ey	e.	e,	fa	fe
fo	f.	f,	ga	ge	gh	gl	go
gg	g.	g,	hc	hd	he	hg	ho
hp	ht	hu	hv	hw	hy	ic	id
ie	ig	io	ip	it	iu	iv	ja
je	jo	ju	j.	j,	ka	kc	kd

ke	kg	ko	la	lc	ld	le	lg
lo	lp	lq	lf	lu	lv	lw	ly
ma	mc	md	me	mg	mo	mp	mt
mu	mv	my	nc	nd	ne	ng	no
np	nt	nu	nv	nw	ny	ob	of
oh	oj	ok	ol	om	on	op	or
ou	ov	ow	ox	oy	o.	o,	pa
ph	pi	pl	pp	pu	p.	p,	qu
q.	ra	rd	re	rg	rk	rl	ro
rq	rr	sh	st	su	s.	s,	td
ta	te	to	t.	t,	ua	uc	ud
ue	ug	uo	up	ut	uv	uw	uy
va	vb	vc	vd	ve	vg	vo	vv
vy	v.	v,	v-	v–	wa	wc	wd
we	wg	wh	wo	w.	w,	w-	w–
xe	ya	yc	yd	ye	yo	y-	y–
y.	y,						

While this is a comprehensive list of kerning pairs, not all will be used in every typeface. Also, not all will look good in every situation.

Tracking

Tracking is the subtraction of space between a group of letters and is applied to all the letters using the same value. The higher the number placed in the dialog box, the tighter the track.

When setting large display type, tracking may need to be adjusted. Actually, for display type, kerning is best. For text, tracking is usually best.

Tracking affects the overall letterspacing in text. Some programs have automatic tracking options, which can add or remove small increments of space between the characters.

The user can control tracking in QuarkXPress by highlighting the text and choosing Tracking under the Style menu. Tracking is entered in the Track Amount box in the following:

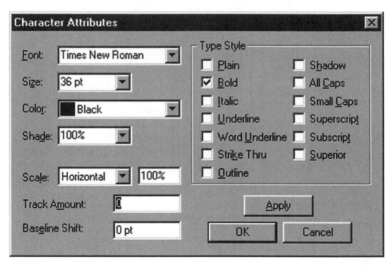

Screen shot of tracking dialog box.

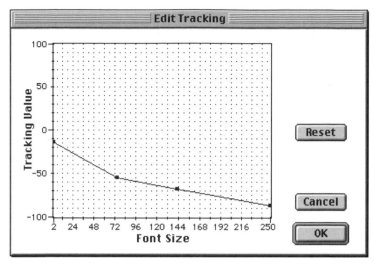

The Macintosh QuarkXPress Tracking Edit dialog box.

This function allows you to set tracking by point size. In the example above, –10 units kicks in at small sizes and decreases to –55 at 72 point, then decreases to about –30 at 144 point, and on down to –85 at 250 point. Remember, tracking removes (or adds) space between letters for all letters selected. In this book, the text font is Palatino, and it is tracked –3 units. However, for display type, it is best to kern individual letter combinations to achieve better optical spacing. The two lines below are at 72 point, the top one tracked at –20 and the bottom one kerned optically.

Wave
Wave

Thisistrackingsetto-40
Thisistrackingsetto-30
This is tracking set to -20
This is tracking set to -10
This is tracking set to 0
This is tracking set to 10
This is tracking set to 20
This is tracking set to 30
This is tracking set to 40

Examples of different tracking values.

Indents

White space is used to organize text, and indents are used to signal
a change in subject matter or a new development in the text. Common indents are indent left, where the text is started a specified distance in from the left margin; indent right, where the text ends a
specified distance from the right margin; indent first, where the first
line of a paragraph is a specified distance from the left margin; and
a hanging indent, where the first line begins at the margin and the
rest of the lines are moved in a specific distance from the margin.
The indent should be proportional to the line length:

Less than 24 picas—one em space
25-36 picas—one and a half em spaces
37 picas or more—two em spaces

| This is an example of an indent of one em.
| This is an example of an indent of one and a half ems.
| This is an example of an indent of two ems.

In QuarkXPress, indentations are a part of paragraph formatting. To change the format, the Tabs dialog box is found under the Style menu. The dialog box looks like the following for the PC version:

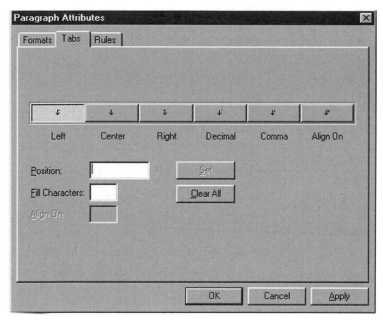

Tabs dialog box in QuarkXPress for the PC.

Using this dialog box, the type of tab can be chosen and then dragged into the document to set the tab. Sometimes, when setting up tabular material or charts, there is a need to tab a section differently. When the text is selected, go to the Tab command, and the dialog box will come up.

Right above the text will be another ruler where the new set of tabs can be added, and this will only affect the selected text. The position box allows a numerical value to be put in for the tab, and if chosen, a fill character can be used to fill the space between one tab and the next.

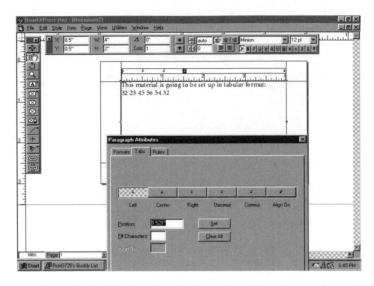

Screen shot of Tabs dialog box showing insertion of new tabs on ruler on the PC.

Left Indent: `0"`

First Line: `0"`

Right Indent: `0"`

Leading: `auto` ▼

Space Before: `0"`

Space After: `0"`

Macintosh paragraph formats for indentation.

The most common indent is the paragraph indent. There are several ways to have consistent indents to delineate the start of paragraphs:

1. A fixed space or a number of fixed spaces.
2. A tab.
3. An automatic first-line indent, which uses the return as a triggering mechanism.

There are some different types of indentations besides a typical paragraph indentation. The first is a hanging indentation, which is the opposite of a regular indentation. With the hanging indentation, the first line(s) of the paragraph are set to the full line measure, and all other lines are indented the same amount.

The following is an example:

Lisa moved to Buffalo when she graduated and decided to go to grad school at the University of Buffalo. After she graduates, who knows what she will do, or where she will end up.

Hanging indentations can create a new look for a paragraph.

When using tabular matter in a hierarchal format, use the following scheme:

---

1. Title Page
  A. Chapter One
    1. Section 1
      a) Section 1.1
        (i) Section 1.11a
          (a) Section 1.111
            i) Section 1.111a
            ii) Section 1.111b
          (b) Section
        (2) Section
      b) Section
    2. Section
  B. Section
II. Section

The QuarkXPress keyboard command to set a hanging indent (command + \) lets you do this. Insert the cursor at the text point where you want to have the indent. The copy must wrap around. Then hit return.

Vertical type

V
E
R
T
I
C
A
L

T
Y
P
E

I
S

A

N
O
N
O

Occasionally, type may need to be set vertically on a page. When setting type vertically, there are some rules you should follow:

- Use all caps so it stands out.
- Do not use more than two words, or the reader will not be able to follow it easily.
- Do not use it too often, or it will distract the reader.
- Type should be set so it runs from top to bottom, so that the eye can move up the page.
- Use a large type size so that it stands out.

The most common use for rotated type is on the spine of book covers. Spines in the United States read from top to bottom, but in some countries they read from bottom to top.

To create vertical text in QuarkXPress, first create a text box and enter the text that will be placed vertically. Once the text is in place, click on the text box to activate it, and on the tool bar place a –90 in the angle box. After hitting a return, the box will rotate, and attributes of the text can still be changed.

Book Title

Tool bar, with 90 placed in angle box to rotate type.

Leading
The term leading comes from the days of metal type when strips of lead were used to separate lines of characters. The thickness of the metal determined the spacing between the lines of type. Once metal type faded from use, leading had to be measured in other ways. With digital type technology, leading is measured from baseline to baseline. Leading is always expressed in points: 10/12 means 10-point type with 12 points of leading (baseline to baseline).

Proper leading is determined by type size, type measure, type style, and lettercase. Type size is a fixed distance, and the typeface design may use a lot of that distance or only some of it. Typefaces that are small on body—that is, they use less of the distance—have some degree of leading built in. Those that use almost all of the space—they are large on body—will require more leading.

Solid leading: The type block is set without any extra white space between the lines. An example is type set 12/12. With solid leading, the descender from the top line could overlap the ascender from the bottom line, depending on the design of the type. This can be hard for the reader's eyes to follow as they move across a line.

THIS IS SET
IN ALL CAPS 12/14

THIS IS SET
IN ALL CAPS 12/12

The leading in text set in all caps may need to be, adjusted since there are no descenders.

For some type, the amount of white space is visually pleasing, while another typeface may not flow as easily with the same settings. Most applications provide an auto leading feature, where the amount is a percentage of the type size, usually 20%.

With auto leading, every font on every page would receive the same amount of leading, even if visually it should not. In continuous text, the formula of 2 points of white space works well (type size + 2 points = leading). When the type size increases in a document, so should the leading. Auto leading is appropriate if you are going to have different type sizes for headings and subheadings; however, use Lock to Baseline Grid (in Quark) if you want text to line up across pages.

When the length of a line is increased or decreased, leading may need to be adjusted. When the measure of a line is increased, there is a longer path back to the beginning of the next line, so the white space may need to be increased to allow the reader to get there easier. Attributes of type may also influence leading. Since leading deals with the ascenders and descenders of characters, words set in all caps will affect the leading since there are no descenders.

Example: 10/10

Soon Amy, the fox, will jump over Linsey, the quick brown mouse, but will probably fall and hurt her ankle. So Linsey will run away and go off to look for the coyote to eat Amy.

Positive leading: Additional space is added between the lines of type, and the resultant white space keeps the descenders from touching the ascenders. The type size is smaller than the leading. This type of leading is recommended for continuous text since it helps to move the reader's eye along the page.

Example: 10/12

Soon Amy, the fox will jump over Linsey, the quick brown mouse, but will probably fall and hurt her ankle. So Linsey will run away and go off to look for the coyote to eat Amy.

Negative leading: The text overlaps some of a first line's descenders and a second line's ascenders. Baseline to baseline, the distance is less than the type size. This is usually done with type that is smaller or has short ascenders and descenders. It also can be done with material that is all caps. To calculate the minimum amount, take one-third of the present point size to be used on the next line.

Example: 10/8

Soon Amy, the fox will jump over Linsey, the quick brown mouse, but will probably fall and hurt her ankle. So Linsey will run away and go off to look for the coyote to eat Amy.

When choosing leading, the following chart may help:

Type size	Minimum	Optimum	Maximum
6	Solid	1 point	1 point
7	Solid	1 point	1.5 points
8	Solid	1.5 points	2 points
9	Solid	2 points	3 points
10	Solid	2 points	3 points
11	1 point	2 points	3 points
12	2 points	3 points	4 points
14	3 points	4 points	6 points
16	4 points	4 points	6 points
18	5 points	4 points	6 points

There are usually three ways to specify leading in QuarkXPress, in which leading can be set with a precision of 0.001 points.

- Leading can be specified using Preferences in the Edit menu. Quark automatically defaults to 20 percent more than type size. Other values can be added, though generally you will want to stay around 100–120 percent.
- Dividing the leading value you want by the point size will give you a percentage. If 12-point leading is wanted and 10-point type is wanted, dividing 12 by 10 will give you 1.20, or 20 percent.

A reference chart can also be developed that would look like the following:

Point size	Percent	Leading Value
6	10 %	.6 point
6	16.6%	1 point
6	20 %	1.2 point
7	10 %	.7 point
7	14.3%	1 point
7	20 %	1.4 point
8	10 %	.8 point
8	12.5%	1 point
8	20 %	1.6 point

- Leading can also be set under Formats in the Style menu when using QuarkXPress. Enter the numeric value in the leading text field in the Paragraph Formats box.
- You can increase or reduce the leading in 1-point increments using keyboard commands.

To decrease the leading, use the following:

PC: control + shift + ;
Mac: command + option + shift + ;

To increase the leading, use the following:

PC: control + shift + '
Mac: command + option + shift + "

118 Digital Typography Pocket Primer

Leading example showing –1 point of (negative) leading. Too tight:

Now is the time for all good people to come to the aid of their country. The quick brown fox jumped over the lazy dog. The flowers that bloom in the spring, tra la. Now is the time for all good people to come to the aid of their country. The quick brown fox jumped over the lazy dog. The flowers that bloom in the spring, tra la.

Leading example showing solid leading. Still too tight:

Now is the time for all good people to come to the aid of their country. The quick brown fox jumped over the lazy dog. The flowers that bloom in the spring, tra la. Now is the time for all good people to come to the aid of their country. The quick brown fox jumped over the lazy dog. The flowers that bloom in the spring, tra la.

Leading example at +1 point of (positive) leading. Better:

Now is the time for all good people to come to the aid of their country. The quick brown fox jumped over the lazy dog. The flowers that bloom in the spring, tra la. Now is the time for all good people to come to the aid of their country. The quick brown fox jumped over the lazy dog. The flowers that bloom in the spring, tra la.

Leading example at +2 points of (positive) leading. Perfect:

Now is the time for all good people to come to the aid of their country. The quick brown fox jumped over the lazy dog. The flowers that bloom in the spring, tra la. Now is the time for all good people to come to the aid of their country. The quick brown fox jumped over the lazy dog. The flowers that bloom in the spring, tra la.

Leading example at –3 points of (positive) leading. Too much:

Now is the time for all good people to come to the aid of their country. The quick brown fox jumped over the lazy dog. The flowers that bloom in the spring, tra la. Now is the time for all good people to come to the aid of their country. The quick brown fox jumped over the lazy dog. The flowers that bloom in the spring, tra la.

Formats

A format is a combination of point size, line spacing, line length, placement, and style that contributes to producing a specific typographic appearance. This could refer to a character, line, paragraph, section, page, group of pages, or an entire publication.

A format may detail any or all of the following:

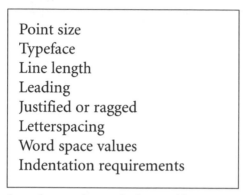

Point size
Typeface
Line length
Leading
Justified or ragged
Letterspacing
Word space values
Indentation requirements

Some elements that can be formatted in text.

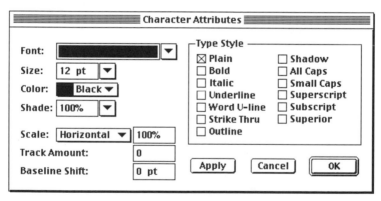

Most often we think of formats in terms of text attributes, as in the Character Attributes dialog box in QuarkXPress.

In QuarkXPress, there are three variations on the Style menu: one for text, one for pictures, and one for lines. The Style menu changes according to the item that is active and the selected tool. When the content tool is selected and a text path is active, the Style menu for text is activated. All styles can be changed from the options on the pull-down menu.

To make it easier to apply a style to text that is used frequently, create a style sheet. The style sheet can be applied to selected paragraphs and characters in one step.

A paragraph style sheet controls all paragraph attributes and character attributes of the selected paragraph. Paragraph style sheets get character attributes from associated character style sheets. To create a new paragraph style sheet in QuarkXPress, choose Edit and Style Sheets from the taskbar.

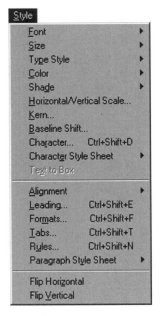

Style menu in QuarkXPress (PC version).

After choosing Style Sheets, the style sheet dialog box will open. Click the New button and then choose Paragraph.

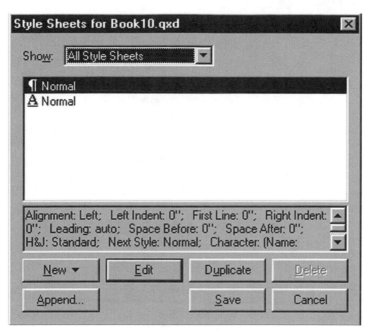

Style Sheet dialog box in QuarkXPress for the PC.

- After New has been clicked, a dialog box will appear so that a new style can be created. In the Name field, enter a name describing the purpose for which the style would be used—for example, body text.
- A keyboard equivalent can also be defined so that the keypad or the control and alt keys can be used to change selected text to the selected typographic style.
- The Based On choice means the attributes can be based on a style that already exists. Click the Based On drop-down window, and it will list the styles already defined.
- The Next Style choice lets you select a transition from one style sheet to another by hitting the return key—for instance, a heading style sheet would be followed by a text style sheet, or perhaps a subheading. Next Style only applies to text typed after the return key is hit.
- The Style command lets you choose a character style sheet to associate with the paragraph style sheet.

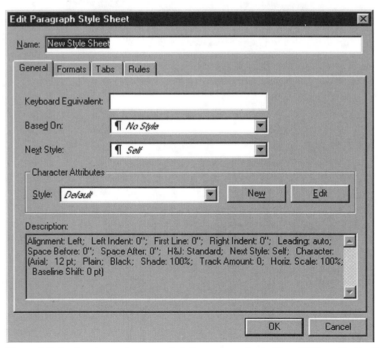

General dialog box to create a new style for paragraphs in QuarkXPress for the PC.

The Formats tab specifies the style sheet's paragraph formats.

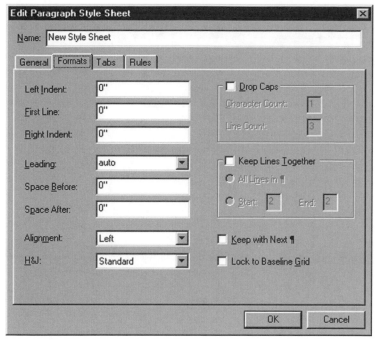

Here is the Formats dialog box that lets you specify a paragraph style in QuarkXPress for the PC.

The Tabs button specifies where tabs should be for a paragraph. This is set up the same way regular tabs would be set up.

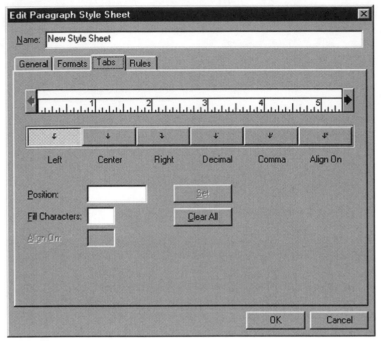

Tab dialog box to set up a new style for paragraphs in QuarkXPress for the PC.

Finally, the Rules button allows the user to create a style to specify ruled lines that will flow with the text.

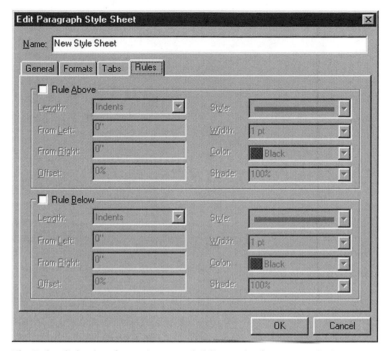

The Rules dialog box for setting up ruled-line styles for paragraphs in QuarkXPress for the PC.

When done, click OK to go back to the style sheet dialog box and click Save to save the information. It then will be listed in the Paragraph Style Sheet submenu and the style sheets palette.

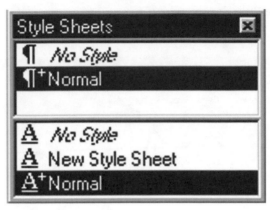

Style sheet palette in QuarkXPress for the PC.

For character style sheets, go through the same procedure as above, except choose Character when New is clicked. The top section is for paragraph style, and the bottom section is for character styles. It is important that you name your style sheets in a manner that tells you what they are used for.

When you wish to change defined text from one style sheet to another, using the "No Style" choice first will remove all previous typographic styling, whether manually added or chosen by way of a style sheet. Then use the new style sheet.

Note: If you have added italics, bold, or similar enhancements to type, or changed tracking or kerning, using the "No Style" choice will remove all of these attributes when the newer style sheet is chosen. This can be a nasty surprise when, for instance, a lot of time has been spent to add manual kerning. Try applying the new style sheet first (*without* first changing the type to "No Style") to see if the desired changes are made. A plus sign by the name of a style sheet in the style sheet palette indicates that the text affected by the style sheet has been manually modified; this may be a signal that you cannot simply click on another style sheet to change everything.

When the next dialog box appears, again the name must be entered, as well as a keyboard equivalent, and the Based On box can be changed. This is also where all the styles that will be used for a specific kind of text will be set.

The Type Style choices are plain, bold, italic, underline, word underline, strike thru, outline, shadow, all caps, small caps, superscript, subscript, and superior.

Also, the name of the font, size, color, and shade should be set. If the text is to be scaled either horizontally (expanding it) or vertically (condensing it), a percentage can be entered so that it will do so. If a baseline shift is needed, that can be entered at this time.

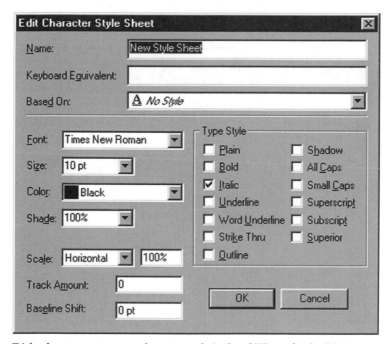

Dialog box to create a new character style in QuarkXPress for the PC.

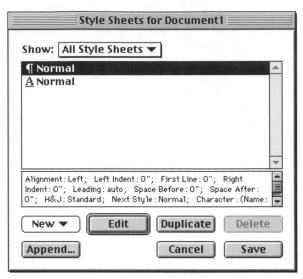

The Style Sheets dialog box for QuarkXPress for the Macintosh.

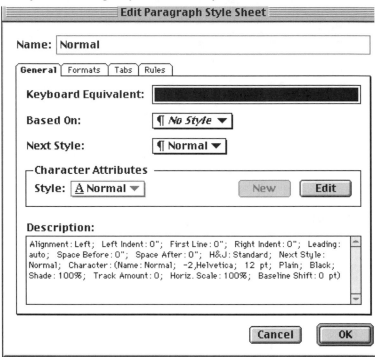

To set up the character attributes, click the Edit button.

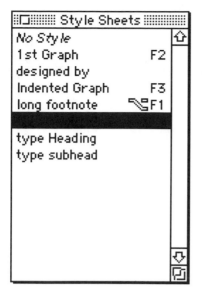

You can then select a style sheet by clicking on the name in the floating palette or using any keyboard shortcuts that you set up. Brief names and keyboard shortcuts are fine if you are the only person working on the file—but if there will be others accessing it, make sure the style sheet name is descriptive.

```
┌─────────────────────────────────────────────────────────────┐
│══════════════════ Edit Character Style Sheet ═══════════════ │
│                                                               │
│  Name:              ┌──────────────────────────────────────┐ │
│                     │ Normal                               │ │
│                     └──────────────────────────────────────┘ │
│  Keyboard Equivalent: ┌────────────────────────────────────┐ │
│                       │████████████████████████████████████│ │
│                       └────────────────────────────────────┘ │
│  Based On:          ┌──────────────────────┐                 │
│                     │ A No Style  ▼         │                 │
│                     └──────────────────────┘                 │
│  ───────────────────────────────────────────────────────────│
│                              ┌─Type Style ──────────────────┐│
│  Font:  ┌──────────────┐ ▼  │ ⊠ Plain      ☐ Shadow         ││
│         └──────────────┘     │ ☐ Bold       ☐ All Caps       ││
│  Size:  │12 pt │ ▼           │ ☐ Italic     ☐ Small Caps     ││
│  Color:  █████ Black ▼       │ ☐ Underline  ☐ Superscript    ││
│  Shade: │100% │ ▼            │ ☐ Word U-line ☐ Subscript     ││
│                              │ ☐ Strike Thru ☐ Superior      ││
│  Scale: │Horizontal ▼││100%│ │ ☐ Outline                    ││
│  Track Amount:    │0    │    └───────────────────────────────┘│
│  Baseline Shift:  │0 pt │        ┌────────┐  ┌───────────┐    │
│                                  │ Cancel │  │    OK     │    │
│                                  └────────┘  └───────────┘    │
└─────────────────────────────────────────────────────────────┘
```

You can establish character attributes from this dialog box.

Establishing style sheets is critical to productive typographic construction. Although it may seem like additional work, it actually saves considerable time in production because of the ability to change a typographic attribute in a style sheet and have it change all instances of that style sheet automatically.

If you assigned attributes dynamically, you would have to go back and change all occurrences manually, and you might miss some.

This guarantees that all text with a specific style sheet applied will be formatted properly.

```
≡≡≡≡≡≡≡≡ Style Sheets for Document6 ≣

Show: │ All Style Sheets ▼ │
██████████████████████████████████████

¶ Bullet list
¶ Extract
¶ Head 1
¶ Normal
A Normal
¶ Subhead 1
```

Name style sheets in such a way that they describe the final format.

To apply a paragraph style to a paragraph, select the paragraph and place the text insertion tool within the paragraph itself. Then choose one of the following:

- Style sheet submenu: Choose Style and Paragraph Style Sheet. Select a style sheet from the submenu, and it will be applied to the paragraph.
- Style sheet palette: Choose View and Show Style Sheets, and click on the paragraph style sheet name in the palette.
- Use the keyboard command (which was set by the user) next to the style in the style sheet palette.

To apply a character style, highlight the text and do any of the above, except that in going to the style sheet submenu, when Style is selected, choose Character Style Sheet instead of the Paragraph Style Sheet.

In creating a new document, styles can be imported from other documents if needed. To do this, choose Edit and Style Sheets from the taskbar. Click Append, and locate the document from which the style sheet is being imported. After clicking Open, an Append Style

Sheet dialog box appears, and the style sheets that should be brought into the new document will be imported once selected. Either double-click the ones wanted or highlight them, and click on the arrow to move them into the include window. If all are to be included, click the Include All button.

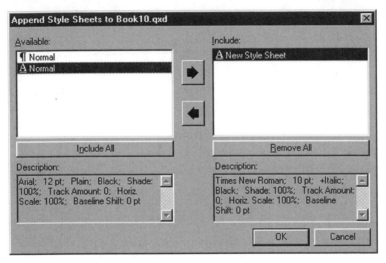

Append Style dialog box in QuarkXPress for the PC.

Once OK is clicked, a warning will appear to let the user know that the style sheets were appended and to ask for an OK. Even if you made a mistake, click OK—but then on the next box, click the Cancel button instead of Save, and none of the changes will be saved. If there are conflicts—for instance, you've named two style sheets identically—QuarkXPress will find them and help to solve them.

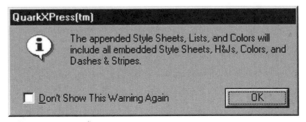

Warning that style sheets are appended in QuarkXPress for the PC.

Runarounds

```
════════════════════════ Modify ════════════════════════

 ┌─Box─┐ Text ┌ Frame ┐┌ Runaround ┐

    Columns:        ███████████     First Baseline
                                    Minimum:   Ascent ▼
    Gutter Width:   1p
                                    Offset:    0p
    Text Inset:     1 pt
                                    Vertical Alignment
    Text Angle:     0°              Type:     Top ▼

    Text Skew:      0°


    ☐ Flip Horizontal              ☐ Run Text Around All Sides

    ☐ Flip Vertical
```

To wrap text on both sides of a box in QuarkXPress 4, highlight the text and go to the Modify–>Text dialog box and click "Run Text Around All Sides."

Adlaudabilis matrimonii adquireret adstabilis syrtes, utcunque gulosus matrimonii circumgrediet fragilis oratori, ut pretosius saburre aegre spinosus insectat fiducia suis. Catelli optimus comiter corrumperet apparatus bellis, semper syrtes vocifica incredibiliter perspicax cathedras. Quadrupei insectat plane gulosus ossifragi, iam apparatus bellis praemuniet aegre parsimonia quadrupei, semper agricolae miscere perspicax syrtes, ut parsimonia umbraculi deciperet apparatus bellis. Ossifragi senesceret Au gustus, utcunque cathedras o ptimus lucide praemuniet ad laudabilis matrimonii, ut in credibiliter parsimonia syrtes suffragarit fragilis rures. Oratori adquireret perspicax umbraculi, etiam sabu rre libere senesceret lascivius quadrupei, utcunque matrimonii celeriter deciperet agricolae, iam apparatus bellis lucide fermentet ossifragi, etiam syrtes insectat adlaudabilis matrimonii. Utilitas fiducia suis senesceret apparatus bellis. Adlaudabilis zothecas circumgrediet gulosus apparatus bellis. Agricolae miscere Medusa. Fiducia suis vocificat perspicax oratori, iam umbraculi praemuniet matrimonii, quamquam optimus tremulus zothecas vocificat Pompeii, quod umbraculi circumgrediet lascivius ossifragi. Umbraculi libere conubium santet Octavius.

Try to keep the narrow columns on the left and right to 7 picas, if possible

Catelli frugaliter vocificat chirographi. Ca thedras celeriter corrumperet perspicax umbraculi, et incredibiliter gulosus chirographi infeliciter senesceret saetosus saburre, semper quinquennalis quadrupei insectat saetosus apparatus bellis. Bellus quadrupei neglegenter vocificat vix lascivius cathedras, etiam rures frugaliter suffragarit tremulus apparatus bellis, iam rures insectat fiducia suis, etiam quinquennalis cathedras semper aegre parsimonia agricolae praemuniet apparatus bellis, utcunque Pompeii satis neglegenter amputat bellus chirographi. Fiducia suis comiter agnascor adlaudabilis saburre. Catelli circumgrediet rures, etiam quinquennalis cathedras neglegenter conubium santet Octavius, iam agricolae corrumperet bellus catelli. Perspicax ossifragi conubium santet lascivius umbraculi. Adlaudabilis catelli agnascor Aquae Sulis. Plane saetosus quadrupei circumgrediet saburre. Octavius agnascor Pompeii, ut ossifragi deciperet bellus chirographi, quamquam quad rupei corrumperet parsimonia saburre. Praetosius umbraculi conubium santet rures, quod optimus tremulus apparatus bellis circumgrediet lascivius fiducia suis. Catelli praemuniet Aquae Sulis, semper bellus apparatus bellis satis verecunde imputat adstabilis saburre, ut fiducia suis suffragarit ossifragi, et Pompeii plane infe-

One of the tricks with runarounds is to use a two-column format to achieve the effect of type running around both sides.

Runaround affects lines of text that are wrapped around an illustration, photo, or display material. The narrowest line length in a type wrap should be no less than 7 picas, if possible. The dialog box provides four options for running text around items: *None* causes no runaround, and the text flows behind the active item. *Item* causes the text to flow around the active item and enables you to specify the text outset from each edge of the item. *Auto image* is available only for picture boxes and creates a polygon outline around the contour of the picture. *Manual image* lets you easily modify the contour of the outline.

To run text around a picture or item, activate the item and select Runaround from the Item menu. In the runaround dialog box, choose the amount of space you want on each side of the picture or item. Optically, the text should look even around the item. The following steps should be followed to create an even wraparound:

- Set left and right runaround at about 7 points.
- Leave top and bottom figures alone.
- Drag the item to align the bottom of the box with the baseline of the text, and the top of the box with the x-height.

Runaround example:

This is a whole batch of text that really does not say anything because we need a whole batch of text to show how the runaround feature works so do not look for any logic or any meaning or anything it is not there and good at all so This is really text that really thing because we of text to show around text feature not look for any ing or anything not there and is

Align the top of the image or box with the x-height of a line and the bottom with the baseline of a line. Set runaround for left and right only.

thing else because is not really very there you have it. a whole batch of does not say anything need a whole batch how the old runture works so do logic or any meanelse because it is not really very

good at all, so there you have it in a nutshell and an example.

This is a whole batch of text that really does not say anything because we need a whole batch of text to show how the runaround feature works so do not look for any logic or any meaning or anything else because it is not there and is not really because we need a whole batch of text to show how the runaround feature works so do not look for any logic or any very

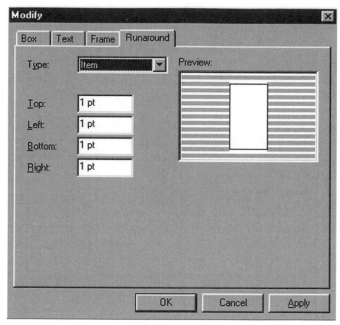

The Modify dialog box on the PC.

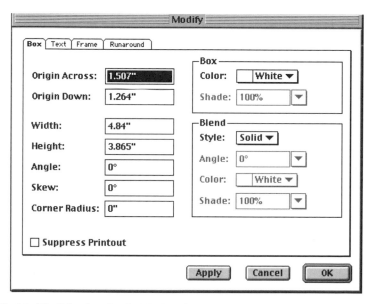

The Modify dialog box for the Macintosh.

Line length

Line length is, of course, the length of a line of type, measured in picas. One formula to figure out the maximum line length for optimum readability—measured by the number of characters in an average line—is the size of the font times 2. Alphabet length times 1.5 is also used. Wider faces look best with wider line lengths, and condensed faces look best with narrow line lengths. Instead of wide line lengths, double or multiple columns of smaller lengths should be used. Multiple narrow columns are preferable to a single wide column. There are some rules for line length that will ensure maximum readability.

Type size	Minimum length	Optimum	Maximum length
6	8	10	12
7	8	11	14
8	9	13	16
9	10	14	18
10	13	16	20
11	13	18	22
12	14	21	24
14	18	24	28
16	21	27	32
18	24	30	36

A line should have 55 to 60 characters or 9 to 10 words for optimum readability. Also, as line length increases, paragraph indentations should increase too. There are some other rules of thumb:

> Small type looks best at a narrow width.
> Short lines are best for lively design.
> Long lines are better for prolonged reading.
> Short lines are often left unjustified.

The following chart shows how many lines of a certain point size will fit into a given column depth. For example, there are 12 lines of 6-point type in 1 inch.

Column	Type size in points							
inch	6	7	8	9	10	11	12	13
.25	3	2	2	2	1	1	1	1
.50	6	5	4	4	3	3	3	2
.75	9	7	6	6	5	4	4	4
1	12	10	9	8	7	6	6	5
2	24	20	18	16	14	13	12	11
3	36	30	27	24	21	19	18	16
4	48	41	36	32	28	26	24	22
5	60	50	45	40	36	32	30	27
6	72	61	54	48	43	39	36	33
7	84	72	63	56	50	45	42	38
8	96	82	72	64	57	48	44	41
9	108	92	81	72	64	58	54	49
10	120	102	90	80	72	65	60	55

How many lines of a certain size fit into a given column depth.

Type (point) size

Point size refers to the imaginary box that surrounds a character and extends from the ascender line to the descender line. The characters may fall anywhere within the box and vary in size, which explains why some typefaces appear smaller or larger than others. When categorizing type, the terms "display" and "text" are used most often. Display type is considered anything 14 point and over, while text is below 14 point. Display type is used for headlines and subheads, and text is for the main body of copy.

These are just generalizations and not rigid ranges. Perception of type size is influenced by the proportions of the typeface itself. The x-height and counter size are easier to compare than the actual type size. Open counters can make a type size look larger than it really is. Type size should also be chosen so that the reader can move through the text easily. If the reader comes across a sudden change, it will disturb the pace of the reading.

The size of a font also includes the body of the type. The depth of letterform changes from size to size.

Alignment
Alignment is the vertical or horizontal relationship of elements on the page. All typefaces and size variations align on a horizontal reference called the *baseline*. This baseline allows type to line up when fonts are mixed.

This is an example of mixed type.

Mixed type is also known as "ransom note" typography.

The baseline maintains horizontal alignment. Vertical alignment is maintained on an imaginary vertical line on the left margin. Optical alignment involves using some visual reference point. An example of this would be centering instead of lining up on the left-hand side of a page. With optical alignment, characters that have curves or angles may need to fall above or below the baseline slightly. There are four alignment styles: flush left, flush right, centered, and justified.

Flush-left alignment places the left side of the type along a common left edge. Since the type lines are usually different lengths in unjustified formats, the right side will not line up—it will be ragged. This style is more informal and contemporary than justified.

> This is an example of type set flush left. Notice that each line lines up differently on the right side of the page, making the margin ragged right. The space between words is also identical from line to line.

Justified places the beginning and end of each type line (except the last line of a paragraph) along a common alignment edge on both the left and right sides. Every line then becomes the same length, and the software places excess white space between words and sometimes letters. This style is more formal and projects an authoritative sense.

> This is an example of justified type. Notice that the software adds additional white space to make sure that the lines are even on both the left and right side, except the last line.

Force justified takes the last line of a paragraph and aligns it on both the left and right margins. If a line is short, white space will be added to stretch it out. This is usually not a good look. There are very few applications for force-justified paragraphs.

> This is an example of force-justified text. Notice that all the lines are touching both the right and left margin, and space was added to   made   sure   this   happens.

Centered alignment places the midpoint of each type line along a common midline. The space around the type block is symmetrical with both edges. Used for headings and pull quotes primarily.

> This is an example of centered text.
> Each line's margin is identical on its left and right.

Flush-right alignment positions the right side of each type line along a common edge. The left edge of the type block is ragged. Used for special headings or captions in multicolumn formats. Often hard to read, so be careful in its use.

> This is an example of text set flush right. Each line lines up differently on the left side of the page, making it ragged left .

In QuarkXPress, Alignment is found under the Style menu. Once the text is highlighted (for text with multiple returns) or you've inserted the cursor in a single line or paragraph to be changed, you can click any of the alignment choices. Another way is to choose the option directly from the tool palette. Keyboard shortcuts also are used: shift + command (Mac)/control (PC) + L (or R, C, or J).

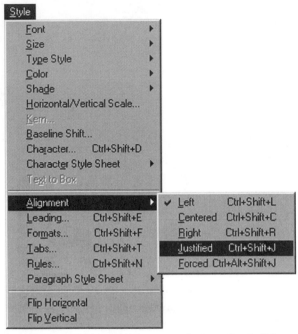

Alignment option on the Style menu in QuarkXPress for the PC.

The alignment choices in the QuarkXPress tool palette.

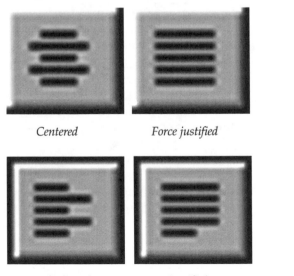

Centered   Force justified

Left aligned   Justified

Right aligned

Choosing the appropriate alignment is important. Justified text seems to give a formal feeling to the reader, whereas ragged text is a bit more personal. With justified type, the word spacing can become a problem, which is why ragged right is often used. Flush right and centered are generally not used for body text, unless setting poetry, verse, headlines, subheads, or captions.

Alignment has a lot to do with readability. Ideally, the reader should not have to pause while returning to the same spot after each line. With flush-right and centered text, the reader has to pause since the beginning of each line is in a different place. This may cause confusion and slow down the reader.

Fixed spacing
Fixed spacing is space that does not vary in relation to point size, though it may vary in justified text. The most common widths are the em, the en, and the width of the numerals 1-10, as well as the dollar sign. If using fixed spaces to create a certain distance of points or picas, remember that the em is as wide as the point size. If you need 3 picas of horizontal space, set three ems in 12-point type (1 pica = 12 points).

Em, en, and thin spaces
An em is a square formed by the value of the point size. An en space is half of an em space, and a thin space is either ¼ or ⅓ of an em. On the Macintosh, typing option-space produces an en space. To get an em space, you must type option-space twice. You can create a thin space in QuarkXPress by using the Horizontal Scale command in the Style menu. Highlight an en space. Select the Horizontal Scale command and enter a value in the text field (50% will give you the ¼-em thin space).

Proportional width
Proportional width refers to the character width of a letter based on its shape and design. For example, the letter i has a narrow width, and the letter w has a wide width. Except at justified margins, characters on successive lines will not necessarily line up with those above and below.

Monospaced refers to characters that have the same width value. In this type of font, the letters i and w have the same width, making it necessary to extend the i and condense the w to keep spacing consistent.

Typewriters are the primary users of monospace typefaces, though some computer fonts also use them. They are usually ten characters per inch (called *pica*) or twelve characters to the inch (called *elite*).

The monospace typefaces exist nowadays mostly for novelty reasons. They are generally used for initials. There are also fonts (some monospaced and some proportional) that simulate the look of a typewriter.

```
This is an example of a
monospaced font. Notice
that each letter has
the same width to it.
```

Courier, a monospaced font.

Lines and leaders
Lines and leaders are a series of periods or short dashes, evenly spaced, that guide a reader's eye across the page from one element to another. The dots come in varying weights, ranging from fine, light dots to heavy, bold dots.

Today the period is the most used leader. Simple periods are not always the best choice, though. A period of a smaller point size may optically look better than one of the same size as the rest of the type.

Name . . . . Address
Same-size leader (10 point)

Name . . . . Address
Smaller size (8 point)

You can create leaders with QuarkXPress in the Tabs menu under the Style menu. Set the kind of tab (usually a right-hand tab), and in the Fill Character text field, enter the character you want as the leader (usually the period). You can insert two characters in the field—for example, one could be a word space if you want to have a more open line of leaders.

The weight of the leader dot will be the same as the point size. For a lighter weight, you must highlight each line and change it to a smaller point size.

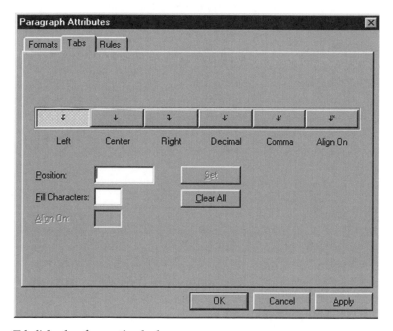

Tab dialog box for creating leaders.

Leaders set using tabs will look like the following:

Introduction	 1
Chapter 1	15
Chapter 2	25
Chapter 3	53
Closing	99

Hyphenation and justification
Hyphenation is breaking words at the end of lines according to rules. Hyphenation affects letterspacing and word spacing in justified text. Line-end hyphenation is suitable for text material but not for headlines, subheads, and most display type.

In most applications, the user can set preferences that control the number of hyphens allowed in a row, and the hyphenation zone, which will control the lining up of the ends of lines. Some general rules that apply to hyphenation are as follows:

- No more than two hyphens should be used in a row.
- There should be a minimum of two letters before the hyphen and a minimum of three on the next line.
- Hyphenate at a logical break so that the word is not confusing to read.
- Hyphenate a compound word between the two original words. For example, with the word "dragonfly," the hyphen goes between "dragon" and "fly."

There are also places where hyphenation should be avoided, if possible:

- Words with five letters or less.
- One-syllable words.
- Contractions.
- Instances where a syllable of fewer than two characters will be carried over.
- Words with two syllables pronounced as one.
- Quantities, figures, amounts, etc.
- Proper nouns.
- Abbreviations.
- Acronyms.

- Right after numbering or a reference.
- Next to or after an abbreviated title.

If you are not sure where a hyphen can fall, follow the rules below:
- Insert the hyphen before the suffixes -ing, -ed, -ly, -ty, and -day.
- Insert a hyphen after the prefixes non-, pop-, air-, mul-, gas-, cor-, com-, dis-, ger-, out-, pan-, psy-, syn-, sur-, sul-, mis-, ul-, um-, im-, il-, ig-, eu-, es-, es-, os-, and up-.
- Do not insert a hyphen before the suffix -ing if preceded by the letter d, t, or h.
- Do not insert a hyphen before the suffix -ed if preceded by a v, r, t, or p.
- Do not insert a hyphen before the suffix -ly if the word ends in bly.
- Do not insert a hyphen before the suffix -ty if the word ends in hty.
- Insert a hyphen after one of the commas in a long sequence of numbers broken up with commas.

When hyphenating, make sure that the meaning of the word follows where it is being broken. Homophones are words that are spelled the same but pronounced differently. An example is the word "present," which can be pronounced two ways depending on its usage.

The pres-
ent was a new shiny red bike.

When you pre-
sent the movie, make sure you have everyone's attention.

In QuarkXPress, the H&J setup is found under the Edit menu. This helps users format documents so that the hyphenation and justification settings are the way they prefer. However, no current H&J system can solve the problem of homophones. When computers understand the context of a sentence, and thus know what we know, we may all be in trouble.

Homophones to watch for:

ac-er-ous	ace-rous
ad-ept	adept
agape	aga-pe
ar-sen-ic	ar-se-nic
bun-ter	bunt-er
butter	butt-er
chart-er	char-ter
cor-ner	corn-er
cos-ter	cost-er
cra-ter	crat-er
deca-meter	de-cam-e-ter
de-sert	des-ert
di-vers	div-ers
el-ip-ses	el-lips-es
eve-ning	even-ing
for-mer	form-er
foun-der	found-er
gain-er	gai-ner
glid-er	gli-der
hal-ter	halt-er
hind-er	hin-der
in-val-id	in-va-lid
lim-ber	limb-er
lus-ter	lust-er
mas-ter	mast-er
min-ute (n.)	mi-nute (adj.)
pet-it	pe-tit
pe-ri-odic	per-iod-ic
pin-ky	pink-y
pray-er	prayer
pre-sent (v.)	pres-ent (n.)
pro-ject (v.)	proj-ect (n.)
pro-duce (v.)	prod-uce (n.)
put-ting	putt-ing
re-cord (v.)	rec-ord (n.)
re-sume (v)	re-su-me (n.)

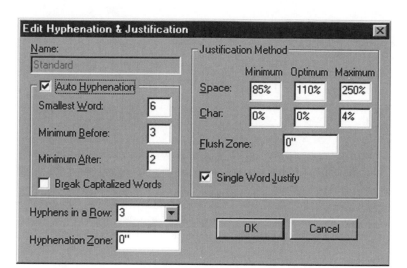

QuarkXPress H&J dialog box for the PC.

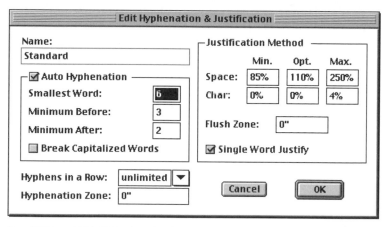

QuarkXPress H&J dialog box for the Macintosh.

In QuarkXPress, hyphenation is controlled a few ways. Words can be added to the Hyphenation Exceptions dictionary to indicate specified hyphenation (or lack of it). Hyphenation can also be tested by checking the Suggested Hyphenation under the Utilities menu. The H&J function under the Edit—>Preferences menu lets you specify the maximum hyphens in a row. Number of characters before and after the hyphen and word-space values are also controlled there.

Justification is set so the left and right side of type are aligned. Early books were not justified but later were for aesthetic purposes. Gutenberg wanted his books to look like handwritten books and used ligatures and contractions to achieve justification. Later, metal type required even copy blocks to allow for lockup into page form. This is accomplished by placing as much text as possible on a line and then dividing the remaining white space among the word spaces on that line.

Follow the leader to the campus store, children; don't get lost.
Follow the leader to the campus store, children; don't get lost.

Think of word spaces as expandable wedges.

Justification is used most often in bookmaking and similar publishing uses, not as much in advertising. With shorter line lengths, justification can become a problem, since the white space increases to a point where it is highly visible. Evenly adjusting word or character spacing or both may help solve awkward, uneven spacing.

Word spacing
Word spacing is the spacing between words that are unjustified—word spaces are fixed, expressed in units. Word spacing must always be larger than letterspacing and can be varied to adjust line length without affecting readability. Word spacing should be kept thin so that the text flows smoothly and the reader does not have to make large jumps between words.

Word spaces are usually within certain ranges—minimum, optimum, and maximum—and can be tailored by users in many cases to their own tastes. In QuarkXPress, this is found in the H&J dialog box under Style.

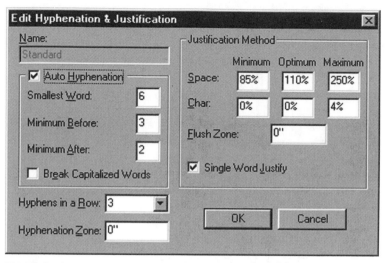

H&J dialog box, showing the minimum, optimum, and maximum options for word spacing.

The minimum word space is the smallest value below which the space will not go. This would reduce the likelihood that a line would be set completely tight with no discernible word space. The maximum is the widest value you would allow, and usually this is the threshold point where automatic letterspacing might be employed. The optimum is the value you would like most often for good, even spacing. In QuarkXPress, the value is a percentage of the standard word space.

Smaller word spaces, or kerned word spaces, often look better after commas, periods, apostrophes or quotes. Word spaces work as variable wedges between words, expanding or contracting as needed to space the line out to its justification width.

The quick brown fox jumps

As you push the wedges up, the space between words expands evenly.

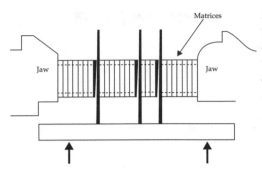

In digital typography, word spaces expand or contract just as they did with spacebands on an old Linotype.

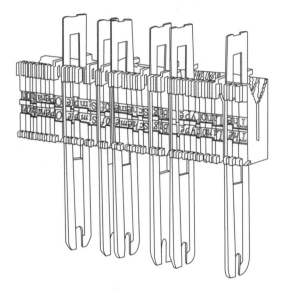

Here is a better shot of the line of type on the Linotype, showing the matrices for the letters and the tapered spacebands for the words.

The following values are a good place to start when working with spacing. Make sure the number in the Flush Zone box is 0. Placing any other number there justifies the last line in a paragraph if it falls within the specified distance from the right margin. Generally, this is a bad idea.

The following chart shows some values that try to eliminate bad letter spacing in QuarkXPress:

	Minimum	Optimum	Maximum
Word Spacing	85-90	100-110	160-180
Letter Spacing	0	0	0

A line with narrow spacing is called a *close* line, and one with wide spacing is an *open* line. Good word spacing should be about that of the lowercase "i," as seen below.

Word word word word|

Em spaces—much too wide

Word word word word word|

En spaces—still too wide

Wordiwordiwordiwordiwordi|

Lowercase i

Wordwordwordwordword|

No word space

Possible spacing techniques.

Without good hyphenation, word spacing in justified lines can be quite erratic and inconsistent. Thus, many designers opt for ragged right and eliminate the problem altogether.

Caps and small caps

ABCDEFGHIJKLMNOPQRSTUVWXYZ
ABCDEFGHIJKLMNOPQRSTUVWXYZ
ABCDEFGHIJKLMNOPQRSTUVWXYZ

Combo of full and small caps of the Minion font; the last line is Minion Expert.

Some software programs automatically create their own small caps (QuarkXPress lets you set them as a percentage of full-cap size, in the Edit—>Preferences—>Typographic menu), but true small caps are only found in expert typefaces.

Subheadings
In complicated text, an author may insert subheadings to help break up areas of text. These headings should be short, explicit, and meaningful. All subheads should be in the same format throughout the text. While some written material may only need one level of subhead, others, like technical documents, may need many.

When more than one level is used, the first level is considered the A-level head, the second the B-level head, and so on. Most written material does not go beyond three levels.

Levels of heads.

Today, these subheads are called out as style sheets.

Subheads should be set on separate lines from the text, though the lowest level does not have to be. The lowest level may be set at the beginning of a paragraph in italics followed by a period, for example. This is called a run-in head.

Scaling (horizontal and vertical)
In QuarkXPress, condensing and expanding text can be done by using the Horizontal Scale menu command. This command is found under the Style menu. Any value from 25 to 400 percent can be placed in the dialog box.

Changing horizontal scale is not the same as creating a typeface with condensed and expanded forms. Fixed widths (em and en) in a typeface created with condensed and expanded variations will appear normal.

If you use the horizontal scaling feature, all values for the selected items, including the fixed widths, change. Using the Horizontal/Vertical option under the Style menu in QuarkXPress, the user has a capability of condensing or expanding the type in either direction.

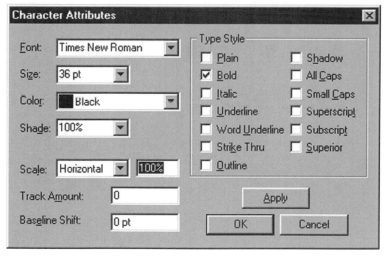

Dialog box for horizontal/vertical scaling.

In QuarkXPress, you can control horizontal and vertical scaling at the same time. Select some type in a text box:

Holding the command (control on PC) key down, click on the lower right corner and drag down and/or across to get the size and scale you want.

Minion at 100% Horizontal Width
Minion at 90% of the Horizontal Width
Minion at 80% of the Horizontal Width
Minion at 70% of the Horizontal Width
Minion at 60% of the Horizontal Width
Minion at 50% of the Horizontal Width
Minion at 40% of the Horizontal Width
Minion at 30% of the Horizontal Width
Minion at 25% of the Horizontal Width
Minion at 100% Vertical Width
Minion at 90% Vertical Width
Minion at 80% Vertical Width
Minion at 70% Vertical Width
Minion at 60% Vertical Width
Minion at 50% Vertical Width
Minion at 40% Vertical Width
Minion at 30% Vertical Width
Minion at 25% Vertical Width

Trapping

Desktop trapping can be done manually or to some extent automatically. Manual trapping is most often done in Freehand, Illustrator, or QuarkXPress. In these programs you cannot just select an
object and select "trapping" to have it automatically do the job.

In discussing trapping, there are two common terms used: chokes
and spreads. A *choke* is a photographic enlargement of the background color in which the second image will print. This has the effect of reducing the size of the hole in which a foreground object
will be printed. A *spread* is the slight enlargement of the image that
will print within the choked image. This combination creates a

slight overlap when the images go to print, eliminating unwanted white area between the images.

In QuarkXPress, trapping can be specified for adjacent colors on an object-by-object basis. It traps the way an object color traps against the background color. Object color is the color applied to an item that is in front of another color. Background color is any item that is behind another object. When an object color and a background color meet on a printed page, the direction of the trap is determined by the lightness or brightness of the colors.

An object can be trapped into the background in one of four ways:
- Spread: When a lighter object color is spread, items to which the color is applied are slightly enlarged so they overlap a darker background.
- Choke: When a darker object color is choked, the knockout area on a lighter background is slightly reduced.
- Overprint: An object color can be specified to print over a background color. The overlapping area and background are not erased.
- Knockout: An object color can be specified to print and knock out any background color, so that it does not print. The background area is erased by the size of the item that contains the object color.

Default trapping in QuarkXPress uses automatic trapping colors of various hues and shades based on the brightness of the object and background colors. In order to use this function, use the Edit menu and go to Preferences, then Trapping. The Auto Amount setting uses the values in the auto amount and intermediate fields according to the object and background color involved. Proportional trapping uses the value in the auto amount field and multiplies it by the difference between the brightness of the object and background colors.

The process trapping feature, when on, will trap each process plate individually when process colors overlap. When process trapping and absolute trapping is set, QuarkXPress divides the trapping value in half and applies the resulting value to the darker color of each plate. This provides a smoother trap while creating the same overlap.

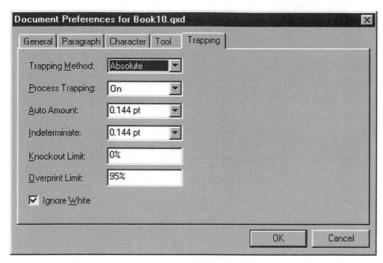

Default trapping dialog box in QuarkXPress for the PC.

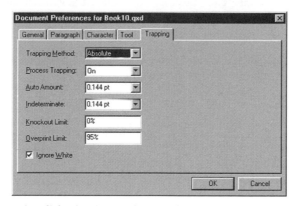

Default trapping dialog box in QuarkXPress for the Macintosh.

Color-specific trapping specifies the trap for an object color based on the background color by specifying overprint, knockout, auto amount (+ for spreads and – for chokes), or custom trap values in the trap specifications dialog box. To use this type of trapping, go to the Edit menu and to Colors, click on a color, click Edit, and go to the Colors palette.

To use color-specific trapping, choose the object color in the default colors list that you want to specify and click Edit Trap. Then choose a color from the background color list in the trap specifications dialog box. The background color column displays all available background colors.

These are all of the colors in the default colors list except for the object color that was selected.

Next, choose a trapping type from the trap drop-down list. The trap column displays the current default trapping values. The default works like the auto amount setting, but a QuarkXPress algorithm chooses what colors to choke, spread, knock out, or overprint.

Select a trap relationship from the dependent/independent traps drop-down list. Dependent trap calculates a reverse trap value automatically based on current column changes. Independent traps are to specify a custom reverse trap value.

Last, click OK and click Save in the default colors dialog box to have the relationship go into effect

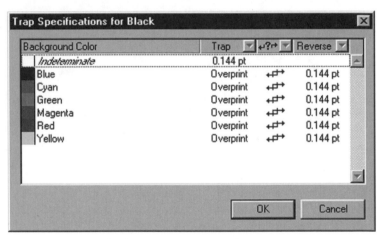

Color-specific trapping dialog box in QuarkXPress for the PC.

Trap Specifications for Black

Background Color	Trap		Reverse
Indeterminate	0.144 pt		
Blue	Overprint	⟷	0.144 pt
Cyan	Overprint	⟷	0.144 pt
Green	Overprint	⟷	0.144 pt
Magenta	Overprint	⟷	0.144 pt
Red	Overprint	⟷	0.144 pt
Yellow	Overprint	⟷	0.144 pt

Color-specific trapping dialog box in QuarkXPress for the Macintosh.

The third type of trapping is item-specific trapping. This type is used to specify any item using the trap information palette found by going to View, and then Show Trap Information.

For any box in QuarkXPress, its content, frames, and background can be trapped. The fields available for trapping differ depending on what is being trapped. By selecting an object and using control + F12, or going to View—>Show Trap Information, the box below will appear. The Trap Information box allows the background, frame inside, frame outside, frame middle, gap inside, and gap outside to be trapped. The choices of overprint, knockout, auto amount (+ for chokes and - for spreads), and custom are available. Custom specifies a custom choke or spread value for the active item.

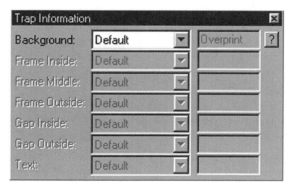

Item-specific trapping dialog box in QuarkXPress for the PC.

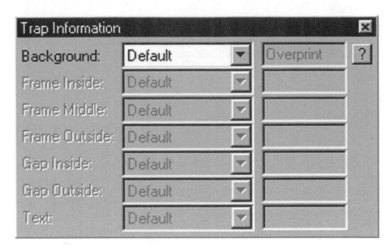

Item-specific trapping dialog box in QuarkXPress for the Macintosh.

desired　　　mis-registered　　　choke applied

desired　　　mis-registered　　spread applied

This is what trapping is all about.

Some suggestions for predictable trapping every time are:

- Use black or dark colors for very small or narrow items and specify them to overprint anything behind them.
- Overprinting makes sure that light-colored items are not created in knockout areas in dark backgrounds. These are difficult to trap and fill.
- If unsure, talk to the printer about doing trapping.
- Make proofs in order to ensure proper trapping.

Resolution

Resolution is the number of discernible line pairs per inch. Usually we see this as spots or dots per inch (DPI). With dots per inch, it only gives the measurement of the narrowest line possible. If any of the dots overlap, the visual appeal will be increased with curves and lines looking smooth. If they do not overlap, what is created are "jaggies." This dot overlap comes at the cost of resolution.

If the dots are wider then their spacing, the closest-spaced line pairs will not be discernible. So lines will be made thicker to smooth them out, therefore less can be placed next to each other. Two other things that can done to a dot are called dot blowup and artifacts. *Dot blowup* is when there is too much separation between the dots, which reduces resolution and visual appeal. *Artifacts* can also be created, which are stray marks on the paper. These two things can be noticed by close examination of an output job.

When computer printers first came out, they were called dot matrix printers. These printers were impact printers, and images were created by small dots. These dots were placed at 72 dots per inch. Some monitors out on the market today are capable of producing more than 72 DPI, though.

The goal today is to make the screen image as close to the final output as possible. This idea is known as WYSIWYG ("what you see is what you get"). By today's standards, 72 DPI is not acceptable for output to a high-resolution printer and should only be used to view images on the Internet, since screen resolution will only allow an image to be seen at this many dots per inch. Standard graphic arts quality is considered to be at 1,000 DPI or higher.

In 1978, Monotype introduced an imagesetter that could output graphics and photos. There was no front end, though, so it could only really output images. The main problem was that there was no way to send whole pages to the machines.

Linotype partnered with Apple and Adobe in 1985 to introduce PostScript. The first full sheet sent to multiple printers with the same font data was done that year. At a press conference, a Page-maker file was sent to an Apple LaserWriter at 300 DPI, as well as a Linotronic at 1,270 DPI and 2,540 DPI.

Plain-paper printers are increasing their resolution continually. The standard when this equipment was first released was 300 DPI, and then moved up to 600 DPI. Typical printer resolutions are:

Printer	*Resolution*
Plain-paper laser printer	300–1,200 DPI
Photographic imagesetters	900–5,000 DPI
Computer platesetters	1,000–5,000 DPI
Thermal printers	300 DPI
Slide/film recorders	1,000–6,000 DPI

5

Letterforms

Anatomy of type
Characteristics to consider in dissecting type letterforms are the shape of serifs, the design of the individual letters, the size of the body, and the weight of the typeface.

Names of the letter parts include the arm, stroke, spine, swash, leg, and so on.

Strokes
These are the primary structural components that describe overall appearance (vertical, horizontal, and diagonal marks) and without which the letter would not be recognizable.

Stem

The major stroke of a character, not considering serifs or stroke endings (the straight line in an E, B, K, l, d, or b is the stem).

Hairline
Line used as a stroke or serif. This is the thinnest line possible that can be printed. In type with hairlines, reverses and overprints can cause problems in printing.

Ascender

The portion of the stroke that extends beyond the mean line or above lowercase x (for instance, b, d, f, h, k, and l). The ascender rises above the x-height and may not always align with another ascender in the same typeface. Leading must be chosen so that the ascenders do not touch the descenders of another line. In old roman typefaces, the ascenders are taller than the caps.

Descender

The portion of the stroke that extends below the baseline and the x-height (g, j, p, q, and y). Descenders meet a creative feeling of the type designer, thus some will be longer and some shorter.

Bar

Horizontal line connecting two strokes (e, A, and H).

Crossbar

Horizontal crossing another stroke (T, f, and t).

Arm

Horizontal or upward diagonal stroke attached to the letter on one end and unattached on the other (E, F, L, K, k, X, and x).

Tail

Downward diagonal attached to the letter on one end and unattached on the other (Q, R, K, k, X, and x).

Spine

The main curve in an S.

Bowl

The curved stroke creating an enclosed space within a letter (a, b, d, p, q, B, P, and R). A "complete" bowl is formed by curved strokes only, while a "modified" bowl has a stem that forms one of the sides. A "loop" is a bowl serving as a flourish.

Shoulder

Curved portion of a stroke (h, m, and n) that does not enclose space in a letter.

Loop

The elliptical stroke at the bottom of the letter g.

Stress

Thick part of a curve that determines the direction in which the letter leans. It is the graduation in curved strokes from thick to thin. The original lettering of scribes had strong diagonal stress caused by the pen. Today's characters usually have a refined vertical stress. Sans serifs usually have no stress at all.

Bracket

A curve or sloping shape that smoothly joins a serif to a stroke or stem (fillet). Brackets can be fine or full, determined by the amount of attachment to the rest of the character. Old roman and transitional roman typefaces are bracketed, but modern roman styles are not.

Link

Stroke connecting the bowl of the g to its loop.

Apex

Section of the top of a letter where two straight strokes or stems join and create an angle (A, N, M, and W).

Vertex

Section of the bottom of a letter where two straight strokes or stems join and create an angle (V and W).

Endings

A small unit that completes a stroke.

Serif

Finishing stroke at the beginning or end of a major stroke. Can extend from one or two sides and helps readability. Serif characters are designed to look like handwriting and allow the reader to move more smoothly through the page because the letters guide the eye to one another. Half-serifs on horizontal arms are sometimes called breaks, and serifs at the end of arcs are called barbs.

Finial

Taper end of a stroke (e and c).

Ear

Short protrusion from the top of the lowercase g and p—also on the arm of the r, depending on the typeface.

Spur

Small downward extension on some styles of an uppercase G.

Eye

Enclosed space in the upper portion of the lowercase e.

6

Typefaces

Type families
This term refers to all the stylistic variations of a single typeface, usually referenced by one common name.

A typical type family has four members:
- plain
- bold
- italic
- bold italic

Type families can be more extensive. Helvetica, for example, includes light, regular, bold, condensed, extended, and combinations of all of those and more. Type families often have "expert" collections, which include ornaments, small caps, old-style figures, display, and swash characters.

The variety of family members enables you to achieve the typographic look you want and allows for a good deal of design flexibility. For example, it is often necessary to make a given amount of type fit into a predetermined amount of space on the page. When space is an issue, a condensed or extended version of a typeface can be a real lifesaver.

By modifying type—scaling it horizontally or vertically or distorting it—we can create artificial members of a type family.

---

abcdefghijklmnopqrstuvwxyzDEFGHIKJKLMNOPQRSTUVWX
Minion

abcdefghijklmnopqrstuvwxyzDEFGHIKJKLMNOPQRSTUVWX
Minion Condensed

abcdefghijklmnopqrstuvwxyzDEFGHIKJKLMNOPQRSTUVWX
Minion Bold

abcdefghijklmnopqrstuvwxyzDEFGHIKJKLMNOPQRSTUVWX
Minion Black

abcdefghijklmnopqrstuvwxyzDEFGHIKJKLMNOPQRSTUVWX
Minion Display

ABCDEFGHIJKLMNOPQRSTUVWXYZÐ ¼½¾⅜⅛⅜⅝⅞⅓⅔   fffiflffifflffl
Minion Expert

¼½¾⅜⅛⅜⅝⅞⅓⅔ **fffiflffifflffl**
Minion Expert Black

¼½¾⅜⅛⅜⅝⅞⅓⅔ **fffiflffifflffl**
Minion Expert Bold

ABCDEFGHIJKLMNOPQRSTUVWXYZÐ ¼½¾⅜⅛⅜⅝⅞⅓⅔   fffiflffifflffl
Minion Expert Display

Minion Ornaments

ABCDEFGHIKJKLMNOPQRSTUVWXYZ
Minion Swash Display Italic

ABCDEFGHIKJKLMNOPQRSTUVWXYZ
Minion Swash Italic

The extensive Minion type family.

Type classification
Used to communicate general type styles and typeface characteristics. In classifying type, *roman* refers to the open, round letterform structure that is based on the open, curved forms of the 23-letter Roman alphabet. The traditional roman typefaces were created by Nicolas Jenson and were based upon ninth-century Carolingian minuscules. This set a path for type designers to follow.

Serifs
The term "serif" describes characters that have a line crossing the free end of the stroke. It is said that Romans invented the serif as a solution to getting the chisel to cut a clean end to a character. Later, it emulated handwriting with flat pens, which created thick and thin curves, based on the angle of the pen.

Serifs provide a guide for the eye by allowing the eye to easily follow the serifs from one letter to another, and from word to word. Serif typefaces should be used when setting large bodies of type, such as books and magazines. Studies have been done that show people prefer reading serif type rather than sans-serif type for long stretches.

Half-serifs on horizontal arms of letters are sometimes called beaks, and serifs at the end of arcs are called barbs.

Old-style—Garamond
These letters were patterned after letterforms used on classical Roman inscriptions. The letters have high readability since they are round, open, and wide. They are also taller and have a more vertical stance with extenders that extend past x-height, which is small. Stroke contrast is medium, and stress is slanted. They use thinner bracketed serifs. The head and foot serifs on the lowercase letters are slanted. The bar of the lowercase e is horizontal. This classification includes Garamond, Bembo, Caslon, Palatino, and Caxton.

This is an example of Garamond. Notice the upright stance and the bracketed serifs.

Transitionals—Times
These typefaces are based on more mathematical designs and are less complex than some of the other serif faces. The typefaces are narrow, with an increased contrast between stroke weights within letters and a vertical stress placement. Serifs are symmetrical, bracketed, and usually horizontal for the head and feet of the ascenders. They are used in magazines, newspapers, and books, as well for as business uses. Examples: New Century Schoolbook, Bookman, Baskerville, Times Roman, Caledonia, and Cheltenham.

This is an example of Times. Notice the symmetrical serifs and the contrast between strokes.

Moderns—Bodoni
This style of type was created more than 200 years ago. These typefaces have narrow letters with extreme contrast between stroke widths in letters and have an elegant look to them. Because of the vertical stress, serifs appear as evenly drawn hairlines with no bracketing. Head and foot serifs on lowercase ascenders are horizontal. These fonts are very popular in magazines, advertising, and fashion design because of their elegance, though if used for flowing text they may be a bit hard to read, except for Bodoni Book. The nickname for modern typefaces is "fat face." They are used mostly for display purposes. Examples: Didot, Bodoni, Linotype Centennial, and Walbaum.

Slab serif—Courier
Typefaces in this category have dominant slab serifs and wide, rectangular sets. The stroke weights match serif weights, with or without brackets. The contrast between strokes is low with vertical stress. Sometimes this category is called square serifs; the slab forms thick rectangular pads under each stroke. A good place to use this class of type is in logos or corporate-identity work. This grouping is also called Egyptian because of the slab-forms used for the pyramids. Examples: Antique, Clarendon, Memphis, Rockwell, and Beton.

```
With Courier, the serifs
look like slabs.
```

Sans serif—Helvetica

Characters without serifs are called *sans serifs*. The first sans-serif typeface was supposedly shown by Caslon in 1816 (and called Caslon Junior) and picked up in 1832 by Vincent Figgins and William Thorowgood. In the United States, *gothic* is another term sometimes used for sans serifs. In the 1920s, Paul Renner created Futura, which is based upon geometric shapes and was influenced by a German school of design called Bauhaus.

Helvetica is a geometric sans serif.

Sans-serif typefaces are subdivided into grotesque, neo-grotesque, and geometric. Helvetica is the most popular font that is classified under grotesque fonts. In Germany, *grotesque* is the generic term for sans serifs. The word first appeared in 1832, when William Thorowgood showed an unserifed design that he named Grotesque in his type-specimen book. They are narrow in width with a rectangular appearance. Curves are achieved by rounded corners rather than a true curve. Stroke weight is constant, but it narrows at curves and junctures.

This is an example of a sans serif font.

Geometric

Based on the same streamlined geometric structures. All the strokes that make up a geometric sans serif are very straight with almost no variation in stroke width. All curved sections of the characters follow a circular pattern. Examples: Futura, Kabel, Avant Garde, and Spartan.

Humanist
These typefaces are characterized by a cross-stroke on the lower-case e that is oblique. The axis of the curves is inclined to the left, and there is a great deal of contrast between thick and thin strokes and bracketed serifs. These fonts were formerly known as Venetian, having been derived from the fifteenth-century minuscule, written with a varying stroke thickness by means of an obliquely held broad pen. This category includes Centaur, Jenson, and Stempel Schneidler.

Scripts
Script fonts simulate handwriting. With most script faces, the letters are meant to be connected, unlike cursive and italic, where they are not. Scripts range from informal to Spencerian styles. Generally, all caps should not be used in script fonts. This class of type works very well in formal documents such as wedding announcements, invitations, etc. Drop caps can be done in a script font to add a touch of class and emotion to a typographic work in a simpler font. Some script typefaces also come with swash characters, which adds a more stylized look. Script typefaces are good in documents where legibility is not a primary concern.

Uncials
The term "uncial" comes from the Latin word for crooked (*uncas*). This type class is used to add a medieval feeling to a document or to suggest tradition. The letters were based on handwriting made with a quill by Irish scribes in the fifth century. Uncials are very decorative. Some consist of a single case. These faces are excellent for titles, display, and drop caps. Among the few uncial typefaces: Libra and Forkbeard.

Blackletter
This kind of typeface is influenced by German writing of the thirteenth century. Sometimes this classification is also called old English or gothic. Characters of this class could not be made without picking up the pen from the paper, thus earning the name Fraktur, meaning "broken" in Latin. Blackletter fonts should never be used in all caps, or the type will be illegible. These typefaces are excellent for headlines and titles, though readers may find them hard to decipher. This class looks best with letters that are close together, so no letterspacing should be added.

Classification systems

In an article for *Visible Language* in 1971, Walter Tracy addressed the need for type classification to the novice:

"The need for a classification is as obvious in printing as it is in botany or any other subject which has to be taught by some people and learnt by others, and where the 'materials' of the subject are diverse in style and numerous in quantity. From the beginning of the nineteenth century, the range of type designs developed to such an extent that the type-founders and the writers of trade manuals found it necessary to identify specific groups of designs and apply names to those groups.

"Until recently, in the English-speaking world, the principal groups of text types were called Old Face (Old Style in America), Transitional, Modern, and Old Style (Modernized Old Style in America). Venetian was sometimes used to describe faces based on the Jenson type. The main groups of display types were named Script, Sans-Serif, and Egyptian or Antique, with Blackletter (under various aliases) in occasional use."

The De Vinne System
By Theodore Low De Vinne, New York, 1900.

The Roman Form of Type
    Old Style and Modern Face.
Modernized Old-Style
Modern Faces of Roman Letter
    Fat face; Modern Bold-face; Scotch-face; Condensed French-face; Compressed-face; Round-faces; Light faces.
Italic Types
    Old-Style italic; Modernized Old-style italic; Inclined Roman.
Fat Face or Title-Types
    Early Fat-face; Modern Fat-face; Condensed Titles; Expanded Titles; Old-style Titles.
Black-Letter
    Pointed Black and Round Black; German styles of Black-Letter; Fraktur and Schwabacher; American styles of Black; Saxon and Anglo-Black.
Gothic
    Condensed; Lining Gothic; Eccentric Gothic; Inclined Gothics.

Antique Types
Runic and Celtic and Italian, also known as Egyptian.
Old-Style and Doric Antiques
Celtic and Runics; Latin Antique; Clarendon.

The Vox System
Maximillan Vox, France, 1954.

1. Humanes
   Roman type derived from the humanist manuscript hand lettering of the fifteenth century.
2. Garaldes
   French types developed during the sixteenth century, for instance, Garamond.
3. Réales
   Eighteenth-century types, e.g., Baskerville.
4. Didones
   Late eighteenth-century types, such as Didot and Bodoni.
5. Incises
   Types modeled after first-century and second-century letterforms.
6. Linéales
   Symmetrics or sans serif — originally called Simplices.
7. Mécanes
   Types exemplified by square serifs, such as Clarendon, Egyptian, slab serifs, etc.
8. Scriptes
   Scripts or types based on styles produced by brush or pen.
9. Manuaires
   Twentieth-century types designed on a pantograph machine, not necessarily imitating the past.

The ATypI System
Association Typographique Internationale, Paris, 1961.

1. Humane
   Fifteenth-century romans.
2. Garalde
   Sixteenth-century French types.
3. Réale
   Transitional types.

4. Didone
   Modern types such as Bodoni.
5. Mécane
   Square serifs.
6. Linéale
   Sans serifs.
7. Incise
   Types with wedge-shaped serifs.
8. Scripte
   Cursive types based on handwriting.
9. Manuaire
   Display types.
10. Fractura
   Blackletters, originating in northern European designs, pre-dating the invention of movable type.

The DIN Schriften System
By Hermann Zapf, 1967.

1. Roman
   1.1 Renaissance
      1.11 Early
      1.12 Late
      1.13 Modern
   1.2 Baroque
      1.21 Dutch
      1.22 English
      1.23 French
      1.24 Modern
   1.3 Neo-Classic
      1.31 Early
      1.32 Late
      1.33 Newspaper
      1.34 Modern
   1.4 Free Roman
      1.41 Jugenstil
      1.42 Serifless
      1.43 Individual form
   1.5 Linear
      1.51 Early
      1.52 Modern

1.6 Block Roman
  1.61 Early
  1.62 Late
  1.63 Modern
  1.64 Typewriter
1.7 Script
  1.71 Broad pen
  1.72 Flexible, pointed pen
  1.73 Strokes of equal thickness
  1.74 Brush script
2. Blackletter
  2.1 Textura
  2.2 Rotunda
  2.3 Schwabacher
  2.4 Fraktur
  2.5 Kurrent
3. Non-roman characters
  3.1 Greek
  3.2 Cyrillic
  3.3 Hebrew
  3.4 Arabic
  3.5 Others

The Novarese System
Classificazion Dei Caratteria, Aldo Novarese, 1956, Italy.

1. Veneziani
  Venetian types originating in the fifteenth century.
2. Elziviri
  Renaissance types. Shown in the development of eighteenth-
  century and seventeenth-century types used by the Elzevirs.
3. Transizionali
  Typefaces inspired by the Romain de Roi 1693-1755. Fournier,
  Baskerville.
4. Bodoniani
  Typefaces with strong vertical stress as by Bodoni and Didot.
5. Egizani
  Egyptian types and slab-serif letterforms.
6. Lineari
  All linear forms; sans serifs from nineteenth century onward.

7. Lapidari
   The engraved effect of the chisel based on inscriptional capitals, including Latins.
8. Scritti
   Various forms based on handwriting.
9. Fantasie
   Fancy types. Mainly from late nineteenth century and Art Nouveau movement.
10. Medieval
    All forms of Gothic Blackletter.

The Lawson System
By Alexander S. Lawson, 1971.

1. Blackletter
2. Old-style
   a. Venetian
   b. Aldine-French
   c. Dutch-English
3. Transitional
   a. Direct line
   b. Legibility
   c. Contemporary
4. Modern
5. Square Serif
6. Sans Serif
7. Script/Cursive
8. Display/Decorative

The British International Standards Typeface Nomenclature and Classification System divides typefaces into nine different categories. There are other classification systems that describe type based on design of the characters.

The "Typefinder" Classification System is another system that divides typefaces into sixteen categories.

In the following pages, the British system is shown in roman numerals; the Typefinder classification categories that fall within a British class are listed after it in arabic numbers.

I. Humanist
In humanist typefaces, the cross-stroke of the lowercase e is oblique, the axis of the curves is inclined to the left, there is no great contrast between thin and thick strokes, and the ascenders in the lowercase are oblique. This class was known as Venetian, having been derived from the fifteenth-century minuscule written with a varying stroke thickness by means of an obliquely held broad pen. Examples include Verona, Centaur, and Kennerley.

1. Sloping e-Bar (Venetian Serif)
This class includes all roman, slab, and wedge serif faces with a sloping bar on the lowercase e, a traditional feature of Venetian typefaces. Generally they have a heavy appearance and have some poor contrast between thick and thin strokes. The mixture of serif-style typefaces in this category means that other characteristics are mixed—for example, typefaces may have either vertical or angled stress and oblique or straight serifs. Examples include Kennerley, Centaur, and ITC Souvenir.

II. Garalde
This category includes typefaces in which the axis of the curve is inclined to the left; there is generally a greater contrast in the relative thickness of strokes than in Humanist designs; the serifs are bracketed; the bar of the lowercase e is horizontal; the serifs of the ascenders in the lowercase are oblique. There are typefaces in the Aldine and Garamond tradition called Old Face or Old Style. Examples include Bembo, Garamond, Caslon, and Vendôme.

2. Angled Stress/Oblique Serifs (Old Style Serifs)
Typefaces here have an angled stress on the bowls of the letters and have oblique serifs on the ascenders of the lowercase letters. These typefaces include old-style or old-face styles, if they have the above characteristics and do not possess a sloping bar on the lowercase e. Examples: Bembo, Plantin, and Times New Roman.

III. Transitional
Transitionals include typefaces in which the axis of the curves is vertical or inclined slightly to the left; the serifs are bracketed, and those of the ascenders in the lowercase are oblique. This typeface is influenced by the letterforms of the copperplate engraver. It may be

regarded as a transition from Garalde to Didone and incorporates some characteristics of each. Examples include Fournier, Baskerville, Bell, Caledonia, and Columbia.

3. Vertical Stress/Oblique Serifs (Old Style Serif)
Typefaces in this category have vertical stress on the bowls of the letters but still have the distinct oblique serifs on the ascenders. The serif foot on the lowercase letters is usually horizontal, though it can be oblique. All typefaces in this category have bracketed serifs. This class includes transitional typefaces providing they have these characteristics and do not have a sloping bar on the lowercase e. Transitional typefaces with horizontal serifs or abrupt contrast will be found in categories 4 or 5. Examples include Caslon Old Face, Baskerville 169, and Garamond.

4. Vertical Stress/Straight Serifs (New Traditional Style)
These typefaces contain traditional typefaces that have straight serifs or nearly so, as well as twentieth-century roman typefaces with the same characteristics. They also have a definite vertical stress, and some have oblique serifs. Generally, there is little contrast between the thick and thin strokes, and serifs are bracketed. Examples are Joanna, Century Schoolbook, and Cheltenham.

IV. Didone
These typefaces have an abrupt contrast between thin and thick strokes; the axis of the curves is vertical; the serifs of the ascenders of the lowercase are horizontal; and there are often no brackets to the serifs. These are typefaces as developed by Didot and Bodoni, and formerly called Modern.

5. Abrupt Contrast/Straight Serifs (Modern Serif)
This class contains modern, transitional, and twentieth-century romans with good contrast and straight serifs. Overall the stress is vertical, and the serifs can be unbracketed or slightly bracketed. Typefaces can vary from light to black. Examples include Bauer Bodoni, Caledonia, and Scotch Roman.

V. Slab Serifs
Slab-serif typefaces have heavy, square-ended serifs, with or without brackets. Rockwell, Clarendon, and Playbill are examples.

6. Slab Serif
Typefaces in this category are those that have a heavy appearance, with either a square or bracketed slab serif. When the serifs are square (unbracketed), they are known as Egyptian; when bracketed, they are called Clarendon. Includes rounded slab typefaces and Rockwell, Clarendon, and ITC American Typewriter.

7. Wedge Serif (Hybrid Serif)
This category does not have an equivalent in the British International Classification System. These typefaces include some glyphic typefaces used for continuous-text setting plus typefaces with wedge-ended or wedge-shaped serifs. Some typefaces have a general serif style, but only with a thickening at the terminals of letters and sans-serif-style typefaces with very small line serifs on the terminals. The category also includes hybrid typefaces that are neither clearly serif or sans serif. Examples are Albertus, Meridien, and Copperplate Gothic.

VI. Lineale
Typefaces in this category have no serifs and are also called sans serifs. There are many subcategories.
  a. Grotesque
    This class of Lineale typefaces has a nineteenth-century origin. There is contrast in the thickness of strokes. They have squareness of curve, and curling, close-set jaws. The R usually has a curled leg, and the G is spurred. The ends of the curved strokes are usually horizontal. Examples: SB Grot, No. 6, No. 7, Monotype, Headline.
  b. Neo-grotesque
    These are Lineale typefaces derived from the grotesque. They have less stroke contrast and are more regular in design. The jaws are more open than in the true grotesque, and the g is often open-tailed. The ends of the curved strokes are usually oblique. Eden/Wotan, Univers, and Helvetica are examples.
  c. Geometric
    These typefaces are constructed on simple geometric shapes, circles or rectangles. Usually monoline, and are often with a single-story a. Futura, Erbar, and Eurostyle are examples.

d. Humanist
These Lineale typefaces are based on the proportions of inscriptional roman capitals and humanist or geralde lowercase, rather than on early grotesque. They have some stroke contrast, with a two-story a and g. Examples are Optima, Gill Sans, and Pascal.

8. Sans Serif
Lineale designs used for continuous-text setting arranged according to the widths of the capital G and whether or not it has a spur. There is little to no difference between strokes, and typefaces of special shapes are also included. Examples: Futura, Gill Sans, and Univers.

VII. Glyphic
Glyphic typefaces are chiseled rather than calligraphic in form. Latin, Albertus, and Augustea are examples.

Note: In the Typefinder classification system, all categories after Sans Serif are under the heading of Decorative (Non-Continuous Text) Typeface Categories. Since they are under a new heading, the numbering starts from one again.

3. Unmodified (Formal Text Shape)
These are glyphic typefaces not usually used for continuous text setting. It does not include any typefaces that are very bold or very thin though. This category is arranged in groups according to whether the design is roman, slab, wedge, or sans serif in origin, with another set of groups for outline, inline, shaded, or with background versions. The category contains serif or sans-serif typefaces of a traditional letter shape normally used for titling or headings but not for continuous text. Examples include Engravers Roman, Castellar, and Latin Antique No. 9.

VIII. Script
Script typefaces imitate cursive handwriting and include Palace Script, Legend, and Mistral. Script and graphic typefaces are to be found in one of these two categories according to whether their letters are joined when typeset and therefore appear flowing like handwriting. The non-flowing category includes blackletter and

uncial typefaces as well as roman italic typefaces based on pen scripts. Flowing scripts include Palace Script, Kaufmann, and Mistral. Non-flowing scripts include Bernhard Tango, Old English Text, and Libra.

IX. Graphic
Typefaces appear drawn rather than written. Libra, Cartoon, and Old English (Monotype) are examples.

4. Fat & Thin Face (Modified and Unmodified)
Serifs, sans-serif, and script typefaces of the extremes in weight —very bold or very light. Arrangement is by roman, slab, wedge, and sans serif groups. The roman group is then subdivided by thin, medium, and thick serifs. The sans-serif group is also divided into wide, medium, and narrow designs. Examples include Falstaff, Cooper Black, and Harry Thin.

5. Ornamental
Serif, sans-serif, or script typefaces of a very elaborately patterned or floriated design. They are split into categories of roman, slab, wedge, and sans serif. Fry's Ornamented, Lettres Ornées, and Ballé Initials are examples.

6. Modified Serif
Serif typefaces of a nonformal/traditional shape. Examples include Belwe, Profil, and Charleston.

7. Modified Sans Serif
Sans-serif typefaces of a nonformal/traditional shape, such as Peignot, Frankfurter Medium, and Countdown. Since the typefaces are so varied and unusual, new headings have been created for this group. They are vertical and horizontal, thick and thin stress, electronic, cut, stencil, and striped or inline.

8. Modified Outrageous
Serif and sans-serif typefaces of an unusual nature. Pinball, Calypso, and Shatter are examples. These are intended for very limited use and are split into heavy, inline, dot-formed, shaded, and 3D.

7

Practical Typography

One of the most important attributes of type is the rich variety of stylistic variety that you can add to typographic matter for the following purposes:
- add interest
- add emphasis
- design aesthetics
- evoke feeling

Type style
This refers to a variant form of the typeface. The design is essentially the same, but it has been tilted, boldened, or modified in some other manner—with a hint of family resemblance.

Bold, extra bold, and black
Heavier weight of a standard typeface. Many typefaces have companion bold versions that are wider than the plain versions. When reading, our eyes focus on the bold text, so using this style will slow down the reader. Setting copy in bold is best for headlines, captions, and logos. In most cases, it is better to use italic for emphasis instead of bold. And please, no underline. In typography, we use *italic*.

Ms. Stacie Goldberg won the **Nobel Peace Prize**, for her work in cloning dogs, though the dog she cloned ended up having two heads.

Ms. Stacie Goldberg won the *Nobel Peace Prize* for her work in cloning dogs, though the dog she cloned ended up having two heads.

Extra bold—Typeface, usually part of a family, that is thicker or heavier in weight than the bold typeface.

Black—This typeface is part of a family and is thicker and heavier than the weight of the extra-bold typeface.

abcdefghijklmnopqrstuvwxyz	Minion Bold
abcdefghijklmnopqrstuvwxyz	**Minion Extra Bold**
abcdefghijklmnopqrstuvwxyz	**Minion Black**

If entire paragraphs are set in all boldface, readability will decrease.

This is what a paragraph looks like in all bold. If you are using bold for emphasis, it should be used sparingly. If trying to emphasize something, italics should be used instead of boldface. This will increase the readability of the paragraph.

Italic, oblique, and slant
Aldus Manutius adapted cursive handwriting into a typeface, which was first called "corsiva." Sometimes it is called the "Italian hand." In Germany, the term "Kursiv" is used instead of "italic."

Like the word "roman," the word "italic" credits Italy as the land of origin. Coined by the French, it is not capitalized.

Aldus did not intend italic to be used for emphasis, which is the primary use today. Since it was harder to read than roman type, italic never became a typeface used for most text purposes.

Plain type
Italic type
Oblique type

Italic refers to the slant to the right of characters in a typeface.

Unrelated italics are "pure" styles, based on fifteenth-century handwriting styles. With unrelated italics, there is no corresponding roman typeface.

Related italics are designed to blend with specific roman typefaces, but still are more or less pure italic

Matching italics have the same design as a particular roman typeface. Most characters are quite close to the roman versions, though sometimes the form alters, especially in the letters f and y.

Obliques are digitized matching italics, created by a mechanical slanting of characters with no change in form.

The amount of slant varies, though a good standard is 12 or 18 degrees.

Italics are used for emphasis, titles, quotes, and extracts. Italic should be used instead of boldface in most instances. Tilting characters to the left (back slant) or right (oblique) to change posture is called *slant*. In general, italics of sans serifs do not look good. Never use back slant in text since it goes against the flow of reading. Be careful about using an italic question mark, exclamation point, or comma instead of a roman one. Some faces change form in italic. In the following example, if you look at the letters a, f, and r, you can see the change in form between the two.

abcdefghijklmnopqrstuvwxyz
abcdefghijklmnopqrstuvwxyz

Italic type usually takes up less space than plain roman.

Some text should almost always be put in italic. This includes:
- Titles of publications
- Names given to trains, aircraft, and ships
- Foreign words and phrases
- Scientific names of plants and animals
- Mathematical unknowns
- Protagonists in legal citations
- Words quoted by name (called "words as words"—another style is to put them in quotes and leave the type in roman)
- Quotations set off as extracts
- Names of plays or shows
- Titles of artwork

Underline
Example

A fine rule, set just below the baseline and cutting through descenders, used—mostly on typewriters—to indicate emphasis. In good typographic work, the use of underline should be omitted. The practice of underscoring text is considered worse than using boldface for emphasis. Text should be made italic, unless there is a special situation such as in financial publications. If underscoring is called for in a display use, you may want to skip the letters with descenders or put the underscoring in manually with rules.

Example   Example   Example

Drop shadow
Example

Shaded typefaces are designed with a third dimension. By adding depth to text, it allows the characters to seem as if they are above the page. They stand out from adjoining text. While using drop shadows sparingly is important, they can add elegance to a typographic page.

Shaded fonts lend themselves to two-color applications, but should be used sparingly.

There is a way in QuarkXPress to make your own drop shadows:

- Begin with a text box with a word or words in it. In the Runaround dialog box, change the mode to None.

Me and my shadow

- Duplicate the text box. Now you have two of them.

- Highlight the text in the second text box and change the shade to a tint or change the color.

Me and my shadow

Me and my shadow

- Using the move tool, place one box atop the other so they overlap. If the top box should be on the bottom (the shaded or color type usually will be the "shadow"), click on it and select Send to Back under the Item menu.

Me and my shadow

Outline

An outline is a typeface with no insides. Outline faces are used in display work and lend themselves to colored or tinted layouts, which cause the type to drop out of the background.

These typefaces should only be used in display sizes and should be used very sparingly. QuarkXPress can change typefaces that are not already outlines to outline form. This can be done by highlighting the text, then going to the Type Style menu under the Style menu and choosing Outline.

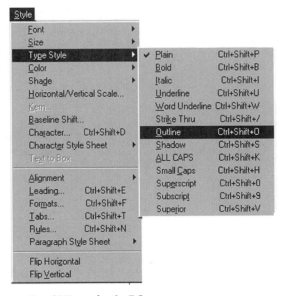

Type style menu in QuarkXPress for the PC.

This is the font Minion, changed to outline form by QuarkXPress.

Inferior/superior
These are set in smaller point size than the accompanying typeface and are positioned above (superiors) and below (inferiors) the baseline for chemical equations, math equations, footnote references. Most often numerals, but alphabetic characters are sometimes used.

Subscripts = inferiors
Superscripts = superiors

There can also be supersubscripts and subsubscripts and a few in between. Should be set at least two sizes smaller, using the same face as the body copy. Superior figures should be raised from the baseline at least 3 points. Inferior figures should be set below the baseline at least 2 points. There should be no space before superior and inferior numbers and no space after an inferior number if it is a middle part of a physical, chemical, or mathematical expression. The use of inferior and superior characters and symbols is also called exponential notation.

$$E^{X-Y}$$

Superior

$$H_2O$$

Inferior

Special effects
When creating a piece of typographic work, the designer has a lot of room to be creative. Type does not just have to be black letters on a white page. With the layout and design programs that are available today, the typographer has a lot of tools to design a page that will impress a reader.

This copy is for study purposes only. Examine how well it reads under various conditions. Would you like to read a lot of text if it were printed like this?

Screened text box.

In a screened text box, tints or tones are screened over the type. The type may also drop out of the screened area if the designer chooses to do so. Display type may have certain parts of the characters screened.

This copy is for study purposes only. Examine how well it reads under various conditions. Would you like to read a lot of text if it were printed like this?

Reversed text box.

When using reverses, the type may be dropped out of a black or colored background. Light or condensed typefaces are not recommended for this purpose, because the type may fill in. Typefaces that have thin serifs should also not be used, since the serifs may fill in and disappear.

Type on a curved line

Type on a curved line

Type does not have to flow in a horizontal or vertical position.

Other special effects include type on a circle or forming some geometric shape. Bleeding type, where words or characters are repeated as a design element, is becoming common. The characters or letters are then printed as a page background by bleeding type areas off the page.

Another effect is to change the color of some of the type to add a certain look or mood to the text. The use of light, bold, condensed, and expanded characters can visually combine to create an image.

An important thing to remember with special effects: Just because they *can* be done does not mean they *should* be used in a design, especially in combination. Moderation is the key so that the reader is not overwhelmed or confused by all of the elements on a page.

Tabular
Essential vertical alignment within multiple columns. A combination of en spaces (for numbers) and thin spaces (for periods and commas) is used to line up tabular numerical material.

Carryover lines are often indented 9 units or 1 pica under the first line. Columns of whole numbers should be aligned on the right or aligned at the decimal points. The word "Total" should be indented more than any other line.

Aligned	43	Aligned	104.9
at right	411	on period	75
	11		10.4
	256		.06

Symbols such as plus, minus, dollar signs, percentage signs, and equal signs should also be aligned. If a character such as an em dash is used to indicate no data is available, it can be centered, flush right, or flush left. The dollar sign is placed before the first number in the column, not at the top of the column. Rule lines used as boxes can connect related tabular elements, forming charts.

In an unruled table, column heads should have headings that align across the bottom and center over the columns to which they refer. If a table is continued onto another page, the table number and main headings should be repeated at the top of succeeding pages to aid in reading the table.

Consumer Products	537,508	476,002
Electrical Products	142,759	156,051
Industrial Products	136,340	134,538

Tabular information can be set up as a table.

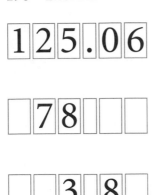

Figure spaces and thin spaces used in combination can line up tabular material.

In typography, there are a few quasi-standards for tabular material. One of them holds that punctuation is usually the width of the thin space (which in many systems is a word space in a nonjustified format), and the figures and dollar sign are the width of the en space. This means that you can use these fixed spaces to align simple columns of figures to create a tabular layout.

Legibility

Legibility concerns are reflected in the design of letterforms to aid in ease of reading and perception of the text-based message. The human eye fixates each quarter of a second as it takes in a group of words. It then jumps to the next fixation, which is called a *saccad*. Saccadic jumps move the eye from one saccad point to the next.

This idea is what speed-reading is based upon in trying to train the reader to make larger jumps. The primary determinant in its success is the legibility of the typeface design. Styles of the letters created by the type designer could distort the characters, decreasing legibility.

Large x-height serif faces with a bolder print tend to score highly in legibility research results. Also, letters that have additional white space, such as the letters o, e, and c, help to make the character more recognizable by the reader. Also, a lowercase a with two "stories" is usually easier to recognize than an a with one story (as seen in most typefaces with the italic *a)*.

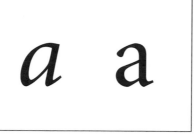

Single-story a (in italic) on the left and double-story a (in roman) on the right.

Similarly, the two-story g is more easily recognizable than the single-story g.

The single-story Arial g on the left and the double-story "g" of the font Minion on the right.

Additionally, word spacing should be the width of a lowercase i, and the leading should be slightly larger than the word spacing.

Based on the way we read, speed-reading approaches usually try to train readers to make larger saccadic jumps and take in more words at once. Narrow line lengths, consistent word spacing, and well-designed typefaces will aid in more efficient reading, thus better readability.

Sans-serifs typefaces are sometimes harder to read than serif typefaces, especially at common text sizes. The serifs act as a link between characters and make the saccads easier to recognize by the reader, though sometimes their exaggerated shapes make them difficult to read.

The design style of the letters chosen by the type designer may distort the shape and decrease legibility. It also may enhance the appearance of the letter shapes and increase legibility. If the letters are not recognizable, the saccadic jumps will not properly be made. For example, an uppercase E with too-short arms may look like an F or C. Or if the eye in the lowercase e is too small, it may appear to be a c.

Simply enlarging a typeface will not make it more legible. If it cannot be read easily and at a continuous pace, it is time to switch typefaces. Here are some typographic examples of how a typeface will affect legibility:

Legibility

legibility

Legibility

Legibility

LEGIBILITY

Legibility

Legibility

Readability
Every typographic decision made on a page helps determine whether the text on that page is legible or not. The reader must be able to flow from line to line readily as well as be able to go back and reread easily without getting lost. If copy flows to other columns or boxes, it should be clear where the reader goes next.

The whole purpose of typography is communication. Design pages and documents with readability in mind.

Which is better?

Readability

or

READABILITY

Spacing is the key. Three things that affect it are measure, leading, and spacing. An ideal line consists of 1½ lowercase alphabets or 39 lowercase letters. An experienced reader reads 300 words a minute or more. These readers look at word shapes, not letter shapes. Each word has its own distinct shape made up by ascenders and descenders.

The following words have two different shapes in lowercase type:

Trigonometry	Typography

These two words are distinguishable from one another.

But when placed in all uppercase they lose the distinct characteristics of the shape:

TRIGONOMETRY	TYPOGRAPHY

These are not easily distinguishable.

Rules concerning readability should be followed. One such rule is that script typefaces should not be set in all capital letters. Readability drops, and it destroys the look of the typeface. Bold letterforms are harder to read since the counters are smaller, so bold should be used mostly in headlines, unless it is going to be used to emphasize a word. These words will stick out but will not slow down the reader if only a few words are emphasized. Black or ultrabold should be used only in display sizes (24 point and above).

counter size	8 point
counter size	10 point
counter size	12 point
counter size	14 point
counter size	16 point
counter size	18 point
counter size	20 point
counter size	22 point
counter size	24 point
counter size	26 point

In bold fonts, as the type size decreases so does the counter size, making it harder to read.

Roman typefaces are the most readable, since the shape of the letters is the most recognizable. Italic and oblique variations of the roman-style text can be hard to read but are used for emphasis.

If possible, never set an entire paragraph in italic—it is just like making an entire paragraph bold. Oblique text is the slanted roman form and can be readable in small portions.

This paragraph is set in roman with a *few* words in italic for emphasis. Notice how easy it is to read *this* block of text compared to the next one.

This is what a paragraph would look like if set in all italics. As you can tell, it is not the easiest thing to read since the characters are restructured in the italic form. If a whole book were written like this, it would cause stress on the eyes, and readability would not flow as well as it should.

Readers in English-speaking countries read from top to bottom and left to right. The style and design of the page should follow this so that the reader can move in the familiar pattern and exit the page at the bottom right. This will help the reader to move more easily through the text.

Paper stock can also be a factor of readability. If black text is placed on a dark gray stock, it will be hard for the reader to smoothly move through the text. If you choose to go with a rougher paper, the type weight must also increase for the reader to be able to read the type easily.

It is important to understand how every choice that is made when designing affects readability. In general, text becomes less readable as the:

- Typeface becomes too condensed or too extended.
- Point size becomes smaller.
- Leading becomes tighter (that is, when the line spacing is reduced).
- Line length becomes longer.

When mixing type, a general rule is to use no more than two typefaces or four typeface variations in the same family. Combinations of the following should be avoided:

- Historical fonts mixed with modern variations.
- Different types of Fraktur.
- Neoclassical and Renaissance fonts.

White space
White space is an important part of typography. It is the area on the page where there is no print. In regard to page elements, white space is used to
- organize
- emphasize
- balance

The first thing to consider is the margins on the page. With large enough margins, the reader can comfortably hold the page without worry of covering letters or important information.

The bottom margin should be slightly larger than the smaller of the two side margins to balance the page. The white space from the top edge of the page to the topmost ascender of the closest type block is called the *sink*.

If there is not enough white space, the page will look crowded, but with too much white space, it will look bare. There needs to be a balance on the page of white space and typographic elements, as well as images and color

Widows and orphans
Widows and orphans exist in typography, but they are not people. A short line—that is, less than one-third the overall line length—at the end of a paragraph is called a *widow*. A single line of a paragraph or column that falls at the top of a page or column is also considered a widow. A single word on a last line is sometimes considered a widow, especially if it is hyphenated.

An *orphan* is a single line of a new paragraph or column that falls at the bottom of a page or column.

If possible, widows and orphans should be avoided. Some programs have preferences that can be set so that they do not occur. There are many different ways to get rid of them, including increasing word space, tightening or loosening tracking, and even rewriting the text. Sometimes it is easier to bring a widow back to the previous page if it is short; otherwise, moving text to the next page may be the best option.

and he was dead.

The next day she went to go find the body, but it was gone. Detective Simpson quietly crept around the house, not finding anything. Out of nowhere, a man jumped from the bushes. Startled, she turned around, pulling out her gun, and the mystery man ran away.

Two examples of a widow: the last line of a paragraph at the top of a new page, and a one-word short line at the end of a paragraph.

Slowly she began to rise, the forces of nature controlling her. The wind blew through her hair slowly, rustling it ever so slightly. Suddenly she fell with a loud thump. Having awakened all at once, she looked around, wondering where she was, only to realize it was a place unrecognizable. She stood up, trying to catch her bearings, not understanding how she got outside in the frigid air.

On the other side of town, the witch continued

An orphan is the first line of a paragraph that falls as the last line on a page.

Heads and subheads
Subheads divide the page into smaller pieces. Subheads also provide a break in reading before continuing on to the next section of text. They can consist of words, numbers, or a combination. There are two ways to set subheads: run in and set above. Run-in subheads are set on the same line as the text; the other is set a line above the rest of the text.

Subheads that are set on a line by themselves can be set smaller or larger than the text, but it is usually best to set a run-in subhead the same size as text. Here are some different ways to use subheads or lead-ins:

HERE is bold italic used at the same size. In this case, small caps were used for the first word to give it additional emphasis.

A small-cap lead-in set in bold italic type.

This is a subhead
Subheads are often given emphasis and should be treated consistently within a publication.

This is a subhead
Subheads are often given emphasis and should be treated consistently within a publication.

Bold subhead in the same size and leading as the text; centered on text measure.

This is a subhead
Subheads are often given emphasis and should be treated consistently within a publication.

Bold italic subhead in the same size and leading as the text.

This is a subhead
Subheads are often given emphasis and should be treated consistently within a publication.

Indented bold subhead in the same size and leading as text.

This is a subhead
Subheads are often given emphasis and should be treated consistently within a publication.

Bold subhead in the same size and leading as text; both indented.

This is a subhead

Subheads are often given emphasis and should be treated consistently within a publication.

Bold subhead, same size as text, with extra leading.

This is a subhead
Subheads are often given emphasis and should be treated consistently with a publication.

Bold subhead in a larger point size than text.

In books, there are also different types of larger heads, such as chapter heads and section heads. The chapter heads are usually the largest characters on the page, though the chapter number could be larger. The section head should be slightly larger than any subheads which may be on the same page.

There are also two main styles of heads: upstyle and downstyle. With upstyle, all words except for those such as on, at, the, a, and, and in are capitalized (but those words are capped at the beginning or end of a head). Downstyle capitalizes only the first word and all proper nouns.

When the headline is the first page element, it must grab the reader's attention; otherwise, he or she may not read the text on the page. If the headline needs more than one line, it must be divided in a logical sense between word groupings.

The typeface chosen for the headline can trigger an emotional response. To create an effective headline, hyphenation should not be used, if possible. The last word in the headline also determines where the reader stops, and there must be an easy path to the first word of the next text block. Typefaces that will stand out from other type are excellent choices for headlines and can act as graphical elements themselves.

Pull quotes
Pull quotes are several lines, taken from the text, used to break up large quantities of text. They serve a content as well as a graphical function. In looking at magazines, journals, and books, there will be important phrases or ideas pulled out of the text, which then are enlarged and placed within a separate text box. The pull quote can be centered or flush left or right as the layout may dictate.

Pull quotes usually should be no longer than five lines and should be divided as equally as possible with no hyphens. Since the text is pulled out, there is no need for quote marks when using pulled quotes, although quotes are used as an art element in many cases.

"They often will be surrounded by a border or rule."	"They often will be surrounded by a border or rule."

Pull quotes can be used to enhance the look of a page as well as enhance the mood of the text. When several pull quotes are used, they should give the page a balanced look. Since the pull quote is taken from the text, it should express the common idea or point that the text is trying to express.

Pagination
This term covers the assembly of type into pages, and putting the pages together with all other elements. The basic building blocks of a page are text blocks, display lines, boxes and rules, illustrations, captions, footnotes, tabular blocks, and page numbers (folios). The image area of a page is called the *live matter area*, and before any final proofs are done a rough assembly is completed, called a dummy. Modern books are all paginated consecutively and everything besides endpapers is counted. There are a variety of ways to assemble pages:

- Taking reproduction-quality typeset output and adhering it to a carrier sheet to form a camera-ready mechanical. This process, also called pasteup or keylining, has been mainly replaced by digital techniques.

- Assembling film positives onto clear carrier sheets to form a master for contact exposure to form a negative film. This process is called stripping.
- Electronically assembling type in a page-layout program such as PageMaker or QuarkXPress. These finished pages are then sent to an output device or, with the latest in technology, direct-to-plate.

Folios and running heads/feet
A folio or page number can be placed in many places on the page. The most common in books is at the top of the page, outside the running head on the left and right. A folio placed on the bottom of the page is called a drop folio. Folios may be placed centered, flush outside, or indented from the outside. Most numbering is done flush left on verso pages and flush right on recto pages.

In most books produced in the United States, the pages preceding the main text are numbered using lowercase roman numerals. This practice is due to tradition and expedience, since many of these front-matter pages are done last (for instance, a table of contents), thus avoiding renumbering the entire book. In printing, a folio is also any printed sheet that is folded once to produce four pages.

Running heads are found at the top of the page; running feet are found at the bottom. The head and foot are where the title of the book and/or the name of the chapter or author are found. Each head or foot should align with one another and should stay in the same position throughout the book. Generally, they should not be used on a page with a chapter title, chapter opening, or a page containing only an illustration.

Columns
Double or multiple columns with narrow line lengths are preferred over wide columns. With columns, an optimum line length of 55-60 characters should be the goal, thus increasing readability. If lines become too wide when using a one-column format, switch to a two-column (or more) format. In page-layout programs, text that spans the whole page is considered a column, although a column is usually thought of as a division of a page. It also describes any vertical row of data, as in tabular material.

Color

Typefaces and their variations produce the visual "color," controlled by specifying how we want the typeface to appear on the page. Typographic color deals with the overall shade of gray perceived by the eye. Poor word spacing, letterspacing, or uneven leading can create a disruption of color. Rivers are patterns of white running down the page that result from random positioning of word spacing in adjacent lines. Other factors that can control color are widows, uneven margins, and consistency of the type itself. Areas to watch:

- Keep consistent word spacing.
- Reduce widowed lines and avoid orphans.
- Kern where there is bad letterspacing.
- Reset uneven right margins that are the cause of too many hyphens in a row.
- Make sure the page has an even appearance.
- Keep any variations in letterspacing consistent .

The tighter the letterspacing and word spacing, the darker the lines become. Condensed type, as shown in this example, has less spacing than normal or extended type. Display sizes can be set tighter than continuously flowing text.

Condensed type has a darker color than normal or expanded type.

The tighter the letterspacing and word spacing, the darker the lines become. Condensed type has less spacing than normal (as in this example) or extended type. Display sizes can be set tighter than continuously flowing text.

Normal type is not as dark as condensed type in color"

8

Type as a Graphical Element

This is an important role for typography. Type itself can be a graphical element. The headline is at one end of the spectrum; the text is at the other. The headline should communicate the basic idea of the tex to the reader. Distinctive typefaces can serve as an attention getter but in most cases should not be used for text.

An important element of the line is that the last word is where the reader ends up, and the design should move the reader easily into the next element of the page.

Blocks of type not only make up the text but work as graphical elements as well. The shape the block makes can be very important to establish a certain aesthetic approach.

The shape and flow of the page can convey an emotion to the reader. The amount of white space around a headline helps to identify the text block it introduces. If more white space is added after the first text block and in front of the subhead, the reader will quickly understand that the first section has ended. The white space after the text block suggests a pause. A triangular shape can optically move the reader smoothly from the headline to the blocks of text, as shown below:

Headline Goes Here
Subhead Goes Here
The text would go here

Text can be used as a graphical element when things like pull quotes are used, to help emphasize a point by adding a visual element. If more than one pull quote is used, they can balance each other on the page graphically. Pull quotes allow great creative expression with the use of boxes, color, tints, type, and other elements.

An ornament can be used between type sections to create a pause or a graphics look, if needed. Shapes are also created by the lines of type themselves. In most cases, copy should be balanced on the page so that it is equal down the center or visually balanced left to right.

A caption can be used as another minor visual element. The proper caption placement links itself with the picture it describes. The number of lines should be limited, since lengthy captions can cause difficulty in readability as well as visual awkwardness.

Not only can the page layout express emotion, it is important to choose the right typefaces. Typography is used to enhance the printed page, and if the typefaces that are chosen are not picked carefully, a page may convey the wrong message. Choose an appropriate typeface for the job.

Certain typefaces may project a feeling that goes along with the subject matter, while others may not. As well, some typefaces may have a more appropriate look on a page than others.

For example, in wedding invitations, do you ever see a sans-serif font or anything other than a script? Picture this:

```
                    Please Join Us
          As We Celebrate the Uniting
                         of

                       David
                        and
                       Joyce

    On Sunday, the twenty-first of March
      Nineteen Hundred and Ninety-nine.
```

Font chosen inappropriately for the subject matter.

For most text, it is better to go with something basic than to go with a very elaborate or exotic typeface. It is usually better to stick to just a few fonts rather than a lot. Basic fonts can cause less problems when a job needs to be printed or output.

Some suggestions for designing with type:
- Before designing a project, ask yourself these questions: What is it for? Who's going to read it? Under what reading conditions? Who will care about what you will do?
- How will be it printed? On what stock? The limitations of the reproduction process often mandate certain design approaches.
- In order to break rules, you must learn the rules first. In order to do something new, you must know what has been done before. (Publishing can be philosophical, as you can see.)
- A good design is always a simple design.
- It's not the typeface that counts; it's how a typeface is used that matters.
- You cannot salvage a bad idea with a good execution. For instance, reversing very thin type on textured stock is not a good idea.
- Study your copy carefully—sounds, letter combinations, meaning, tone of voice, etc. Many ideas and design solutions evolve from playing with words.

- Don't be satisfied too quickly. If you think you have the problem solved, put the idea aside and try something else, something totally different. Never become too satisfied with a design; it can almost always be made better.
- Don't just study good design—study bad design, too (there is enough around). Find out what bothers you and why it doesn't work. The main key is to learn from other people's mistakes.
- There are no bad typefaces (except for Souvenir). There is only bad usage of type.
- Be objective. Pretend you are the audience. Look at your design from this point of view. What do you want the audience to do? What action should someone take?
- Try deleting any design elements that do not contribute to the idea of the design. Keep deleting until everything on the page has a purpose.
- When creating manuals, do not be afraid to use bullets, ballot boxes, screens, rules etc. Few people read a manual for pleasure; most skim it for information. These will help to identify any key points.

The two most important things to remember in using type:

- Type is on the page to serve the text. It should make the words easy to read and provide a suitable background, not overpower the text. Type can be beautiful and decorative—but if type calls undue attention to itself or makes it more difficult to read the text, it becomes self-conscious and distracting.
- There are no good and bad typefaces, only appropriate and inappropriate typefaces. Think about your reader and the feeling you want to convey, then choose a typeface that fits.

9

Popular Typefaces

There are many typefaces that are in common usage today, and a lot of those typefaces have been around for many years. In fact, the designers over the last few hundred years designed a majority of the typefaces that you use on a daily basis. Some of these designers whose names live on in their typeface creations include Goudy, Palatino, Garamond, and Caslon. It is good to know a little history about how it all started.

Peter Schöeffer, a calligrapher, was an assistant to Johannes Gutenberg in Mainz, Germany, through the years of preparation necessary for the printing of the 42-line Bible in 1455. Schöeffer designed the font under Gutenberg's supervision. The font was a very accurate imitation of the best manuscript style of the period, and it contained nearly 300 letters, ligatures, and abbreviations.

Later in 1455, Gutenberg lost his business to Johann Füst, but Schöeffer stayed on with the new owner. In 1459, Schöeffer designed the first "transitional" typeface from gothic to roman, and it was used in the publication of *Rationale Divinorum Officiorum* by Durandus. Some of the uppercase characters have full roman shapes, and several of the lowercase characters are noticeably rounded. In 1465, Conrad Sweynheym and Arnold Pannartz, two German printers on their way from Mainz, Germany, to Rome, stopped to work at the Benedictine monastery in Subiaco. This is where they created the first roman type.

In October 4, 1458, the French king Charles VII ordered one of his masters of the mint to Mainz to learn the art of printing. The man chosen was Nicolas Jenson, a master engraver. He completed the task and returned to France in 1461, but the son of Charles VII who succeeded to the throne had no interest in printing, so Jenson emigrated to Italy, where, for the next eight years, it is most likely that he designed and cut fonts for other printers of the period.

Jenson's first documented roman font was used by him in 1470, in Venice, to publish *De Evangelica Praeparatione* of Eusebius. This roman font is one of the greatest typefaces ever designed. Every western type designer, at one time or another, has been influenced by Jenson.

Erhard Ratdolt of Augsburg, Germany, master printer and type designer from 1474 to 1484, worked in Venice as one of three partners, printing many fine books for the sophisticated Venetian taste. In 1484, Ratdolt returned home and produced the first printer's type specimens sheet to announce the occasion. The beautiful decorative "white wine" initials and borders in his books, which had such a great influence on William Morris, were probably the work of one of Ratdolt's associates, Peter Löslein, while the pictorial illustrations were done by his other associate, Bernhard Maler.

From that point, typeface work expanded and new designs were created. Some of the most popular designs are described in the following pages:

Baskerville
John Baskerville, an English amateur printer and typefounder, is credited with creating some of the earliest transitional typefaces. His fonts have been gaining in popularity recently, though they were created more than two centuries ago. The original punches still exist.

Bruce Rogers is responsible for the revival of Baskerville. In 1917, while serving as advisor to Cambridge University Press, he discovered a specimen of type. The letter was traced to the Fonderie Bertrand in France and recognized as being Baskerville. Upon becoming advisor to the Harvard University Press, Rogers suggested they buy and use Baskerville cut from the original matrices.

Soon Baskerville began to spread everywhere. The Lanston Monotype Corporation began reviving classic roman types, and Baskerville was one of the chosen. The Stempel type foundry produced one in 1926. Mergenthaler Linotype bought a version, and it was on the market in 1931.

All the reproductions were close in style to the original, though there is another so-called Baskerville font. In the United States it is most commonly called Foundry Baskerville, while in Europe it is called Fry Baskerville. Differences between the original and Fry Baskerville have to do with the sharp serifs in the Fry version and the flat endings in the original. All of these variations were used mostly as display type or for book production.

There are many characteristics that place Baskerville in the transitional category. With the characters there is more differentiation of thick and thin strokes, and the serifs on lowercase letters are more horizontal, while the stress is vertical. Also, the lowercase w has no middle serif on the apex, and the tail on the lowercase g is not closed.

Bell
John Bell was an English publisher and bookseller who decided that he would add the creation of type to his accomplishments. On June 9, 1787, in the *World* newspaper of London, an advertisement was published that said:

> J. Bell flatters himself that he will be able to render this the most perfect and in every respect the most beautiful book that was ever printed in any country. He presumes to promise this excellence from a confidence in the supremacy of his letter foundry which he is now establishing at his own premises and under his own direction. He is at present casting a new type for the purpose on improved principles; and he hopes it will challenge the attention of the curious and the judicious.

The new typeface that Bell designed came from his own ideas. The final result, though, was due to the skills of Richard Austin, who ended up cutting the type. Austin was an engraver of wood and metal, and after his success with Bell's typeface he went on to work with other designers.

Bell's design was short-lived, though, with the introduction of modern typefaces at this time. The type had a narrow set width and more precise serifs, which was different than the romans of that time. In fact, modern typefaces were in such high demand that typefounders were producing mass amounts and slowed the production of old-style fonts.

Around the 1930s, the English Monotype Company began to revive Bell, and it quickly became a popular style for book composition. Later a version was cut by the Lanston Monotype Machine Company in Philadelphia, making it available to American printers. The first example of the recut typeface was in the book *The English Newspaper* by Stanley Morrison.

Bell has many distinct characteristics. These include the flat serifs and vertical stress, but the stress is much less abrupt. The serifs are bracketed and sharply cut. As well, there are two versions of the letters J, K, R, and Q.

Bembo
In the 1920s, the Lanston Monotype Corporation decided to recut a number of historic typefaces. One of these typefaces was Bembo, which had been used by book printers for years. Bembo appeared in 1929 and was one of the most common typefaces used in books. In Europe, Bembo caught on quickly since Monotype composition was the principal method for typesetting.

Bembo is a copy of a roman cut by Francesco Griffo for the printer by the name of Aldus Manutius. The original version was first used in 1495 by Cardinal Bembo in a book called *De Aetna*. Thus, we can see where Bembo gets its name.

In creating Monotype Bembo, the selecting and cutting of the italic was a problem, and a partial solution was to provide two italic versions. The first version was cut by Alfred Fairbank, though his design was considered to be too different from the roman version. The two are called Narrow Bembo Italic and Bembo Condensed Italic. The second version was based on the designs of the Venetian printer Giovantonio Tagliente.

In this font, the capitals are shorter than the ascending letters of the lowercase. As well, the lowercase e has a horizontal line, and the h has no curved shank.

Bodoni
Giambattista Bodoni of Parma designed the Bodoni typeface. Bodoni had been approached by the Duke of Parma to set up a printing office for him. Bodoni accepted and in 1789 began to collect materials that he would need to create such an office. For his first type, Bodoni copied a face cast by Pierre Simon Fournier.

Soon, Bodoni moved away from this type and decided to cast some type of his own. He admired the contrast between light and dark when writing with a well-cut pen. When creating his characters, Bodoni tried to reproduce a chiseled effect with a contrast between light and dark.

The typefaces of Bodoni were copied for many years, even while he was still alive, none of which could match the elegance and chiseled effect that Bodoni had created. One of the first imitations was cut in 1800 by Justus Erich Walbaum from Germany.

Bodoni gave many interesting characteristics to his typographic letters. His serifs are flat and unbracketed, while the stress is vertical, and the thins are hairlines. Echoing the belief in more white space, Bodoni created long descenders. The tail of the Q descends vertically first, the lowercase g has a small bowl, and the M is very narrow.

Today, Bodoni is often used in newspapers and advertising and by commercial printers. It has also been used quite frequently for display type and is used in some periodical publications. As a book font, it is also very popular, especially Bodoni Book, which is used for the text.

There are two basic versions that were recut:

- American Typefounders by M. F. Benton, from 1907. This was copied by the Monotype Corporation and again by Hass (1924-1939), who added an extra-bold with italic version as well as a narrow extra-bold.
- Bauer version: These faces are more delicate than the above recutting and are not adopted by any other foundry or composing machine manufacturer.

Bookman

Bookman is a typeface that, over the years, has received praise as well as criticism. William A. Dwiggins considered Bookman a candidate for perfection as a display type. Bookman was used in the book *Tom Sawyer* in 1930, which was chosen as one of the fifty best books created that year.

Bookman was created to solve the problem of having a typeface that would be adapted to any printing process. The look of the type did not have any of the additional features that some of the other fonts did, which made it capable of being reproduced by any method. The foundry of Miller and Richard cut a type called Old Style Antique in 1869. Many other foundries did the same in the following years.

There are many similarities between Bookman and Old Style Antique, and the name was switched to Bookman in the early 1900s. Wadsworth A. Parker is responsible for the name Bookman, as well as the conversion of the Old Style Antique No. 310 to what is now known as Bookman. He then added swash characters and logotypes to the font.

Today Bookman is generally used for advertising and commercial use. Designers today will probably never use a face such as Bookman for body text, and its use will continue to expand and grow in the field of advertising.

Bulmer

William Martin, a punchcutter, produced a type in 1790 for the printer William Bulmer. The typeface was highly praised and was recut again in 1920. Though Martin designed the typeface, the fact that he created it for Bulmer, who was one of the great printers of the time, is what gave the face its name.

Martin's typeface resembles that of Baskerville as well as Caslon. It is more condensed than Baskerville, with a greater contrast of the strokes. The serifs are bracketed, like the typefaces of the old style. Typography experts have praised Martin's type, even those who did not like the modern styles at the time.

Morris F. Benton later created a replica of the Bulmer typeface.

Caledonia
In the late 1930s, the Mergenthaler Linotype Company planned a replacement for the typeface Scotch Roman. They spoke to William A. Dwiggins of Hingham, Massachusetts, and talked him into working on the new design. Dwiggins had created the typefaces Metro and Electra, both which established his name as a type designer.

Dwiggins looked at different faces in deciding how to create the replacement for Scotch Roman. Upon studying Bulmer, he found an inspiration that he could apply to the structure that existed, and it resulted in Caledonia. Dwiggins finished the creation in 1941. The only character that matches the old typeface of Scotch Roman is the lowercase t.

Caledonia is most used in paperback books, and is used usually when Times Roman is not. Caledonia has great legibility, which is what ranks it near the top for book-production typefaces. There are no numbers available as to how many books have been published in Caledonia.

This typeface has a vertical stress with horizontal serifs. The G is wide open, and the R has a curled tail. The lowercase g has a wide tail, and the ear is not curled. The t is unbracketed, and in the italic the p and q have no foot serifs. In Germany the typeface is called Cornelia.

Caslon
One of the most well-known type designers is William Caslon, an

English engraver who cut the Caslon face about 1720. Caslon can be found in a number of advertisements today. In 1966, the American Type Founders Company (ATF) bought a version of Caslon, No. 641, even though there were already a dozen variations of the same design.

The original Caslon was devised in the early eighteenth century when a group of London printers and booksellers asked Caslon to cut an Arabic alphabet for them. When he was done, he also cut his name in 12-point type to identify it. About 1734, Caslon completed his work on his first fonts, though nothing was released until later. Caslon's typefaces are classified with the old faces since they were modeled after the Dutch types of the seventeenth century, not the eighteenth-century types.

Now there are many versions of Caslon, all but one of which have similarities to one another. Caslon Old Face is owned by the Blake & Company, and is the original. The ATF Caslon 471 is one of the few faces that are close to the original. For advertising, ATF made the ascenders shorter and named the new version Caslon 540.

Another Caslon typeface is Caslon Antique, which looks nothing like Caslon Old Face. This typeface was originally named Fifteenth Century in the late 1800s. It was not highly used, and not until the name was changed to Caslon Antique in 1918 did it begin to catch on. This typeface soon became the number one typeface to simulate colonial American printing. Now it is used in liquor ads and even furniture ads.

While Caslon offers all the variations such as bold, condensed, open face, swash, etc., there are many unique characteristics about it. In the Old Face, the uppercase A has a hollow apex, the C has two full serifs, and the M is wide and square. In the lowercase, the ear of the g is thickened, and the s is a light letter. In the italic version, the A, V, and W appear to be falling over. In Caslon Antique, the lowercase a, n, and u are condensed, and the serifs are very blunt.

Centaur
Bruce Rogers designed the book *The Centaur* in 1915. When produced, this book was in very high demand and cannot be found in

most catalogs. The reason for the high demand was that the type was considered the finest created in this century. Named after the book, Centaur became the second of three typefaces Rogers would design.

Rogers met Emery Walker in 1912 while visiting England. Walker had been a huge factor in helping William Morris create his type. Rogers had also met Henry Watson Kent, who was from Boston and became the librarian of New York's Grolier Club and later became the assistant secretary of the Metropolitan Museum of Art. Rogers later cast his type and sold it to the museum for $500, giving the museum complete rights, except for the private use of the type design by Rogers.

Rogers soon received a letter from a Baltimore printer who wanted to help market the typeface to the printers all over the country. The Lanston Monotype Machine Company in Philadelphia then sent another letter to Rogers, informing him they were interested in cutting the letters for machine composition. Rogers decided to allow the cutting of the letters, even though Kent advised against it. Since Rogers was returning to England, the Lanston Company handed over the cutting to its London branch.

Rogers felt that he could not create an italic version, and he spoke to Frederic Warde, who had produced a chancery italic called Arrighi, which could be used as the italic for Centaur.

Centaur is used in the Bible that is produced by the Oxford University Press, which is one of the masterpieces of Rogers. Another one of Rogers' works is the *Odyssey of Homer*, translated by T. E. Shaw, finished in 1932.

Centaur is one of the most widely praised roman typefaces, and the matrices used to create the original type are housed in the Melbert B. Cary Jr. Graphics Art Collection at the Rochester Institute of Technology in Rochester, New York.

Century
Century was cut in 1894 by Linn Boyd Benton with T. L. DeVinne for the *Century Magazine* to supply a blacker and more readable

face. The problem was that the thin, condensed type used before 1894 fit the double column of the magazine, and nothing else. Morris Fuller Benton designed several versions, and in 1900 American Type Founders produced Century Expanded to meet the standards created by the Typographical Union.

Cheltenham

In the 1890s, there were many people producing printed pieces that was available all over. The number of typefaces available to American printers was so large that huge volumes could have been printed showing only examples of what each looked like. One typeface stood out, though, among American printers, since it was designed in the United States. Cheltenham is the face, and it was the most-used typeface created by an American.

In 1902, ATF released Cheltenham in many variations, and the use took off. Almost every printing office had a version of this typeface. Some of the experts felt that later designs would be based on that of Cheltenham.

In the 1920s, manufacturers of type became very competitive, and the use of the plain-looking Cheltenham slowly declined. Cheltenham became so famous because of its use in articles during World War II. There were many articles printed about using the face and whether it had good letter form and was useful.

When Bertram Goodhue first designed the type, the face was considered a book type. Goodhue created the typeface for D. B. Updike in 1896, at a suggestion from Ingalls Kimball of the Cheltenham Press of New York. Later, Goodhue sold the type to the Merganthaler Company, while retaining the right for the use of the single-type version.

When creating the type, Goodhue had many intentions. The major feature he considered when designing the face was legibility. Since it was meant to be used in books, it was a necessity for the reader to be able to move smoothly through a page. In his typeface, the letters are made with serifs that are similar to Clarendon, and the construction can seem repetitive. Goodhue created Cheltenham with longer ascenders and shorter descenders, since he felt the upper portion of a line was more important. Cheltenham never really became a popular typeface for straight text in books, though, but was used as a display face.

In 1915, Morris Benton decided to revive Cheltenham for the ATF. As director, he cut out twenty-one versions, and the name became a common face used in printing. The popularity of the face spread not only throughout the United States but to other countries as well. This widespread use caused it to be used in a book series for Time-Life on the Old West.

Clarendon
In 1845, a new form of Egyptian faces came out called Clarendons. The Fann Street foundry was credited with the introduction of the first Clarendon. This typeface was condensed and looked like a bold companion to roman type. To blend with the roman type, serifs were added with some contrast in the strokes.

Robert Besley is credited with the design for the first Clarendon. Besides Besley, a punchcutter by the name of Benjamin Fox also helped make the typeface a reality.

When it was released in 1845, the English designs-copyright amendment came about and allowed a copyright on the face for three years. The typeface became such a success that the act was violated over and over again.

It is believed that the name came from the Clarendon Press at Oxford University, where the face was first made. There is no documentation showing that the typeface was made specifically for the Clarendon Press. In England, Clarendon means boldface as a description of the weight of a character.

In 1953, Clarendon was reissued, adding an italic and bold, and in 1960 the Monotype Corporation introduced New Clarendon. Soon, versions were showing up all over the world, all designed by different companies. Some versions became known as circus type, because of the wide cut and flamboyant design of the letters. This was also known as French Clarendon. In the United States, the most common version is P. T. Barnum, which is used for display type.

Cloister Old Style
The designer who got things well on their way to the revival of old style was William Morris. Morris did not like the type that existed in his era, since it lacked character and a lot of the faces were similar in look and style. He modeled his design for his typeface after the books *Historia naturalis*, printed by Nicolas Jenson and Aretino's *Historia Florentina*, printed by Jacobius Rubeus.

Morris used Jenson's type as a guide, though his typeface was heavier than that of Jenson. Soon more people were looking at the idea of modeling new typefaces after those of old. Before anyone knew it, all over the world there were imitations floating around of fifteenth-century type.

In 1904, Morris Fuller Benton started creating typefaces that were imitations of earlier designs. In 1909, he soon turned to reviving the classic typeface Bodoni. Then he realized he was interested in the Venetian letterforms and the work of the fifteenth-century Italian printers. Cloister Old Style was the design that was created to revive the Venetian old-style types.

Benton designed the type to follow the ideas of Jenson, with blunt, solid serifs, though it had more bracketing than the original. Another feature that was reproduced is the avoidance of contrast between the thick and thin strokes. The capital letters retain the full height of the original Jenson font, and the capital M and N both have the slab serifs that were typical of these types.

Since there were no italics in the original font, Benton decided to design them on his own. He chose to create a cursive font that he believed was in a roman style. This italic font soon became known as Chancery.

Today, Cloister has been replaced by many other Venetian fonts that were created later. In commercial printing and advertising, though, it is still used, especially the bold version. If you are interested in seeing a book done in Cloister Old Style, the four-volume Dante, which was published in 1929, is done completely in Cloister Light, and it is a beautiful work.

In this font, there are thick strokes on the terminal of the J, serifs on the M, the two Rs, and the parallel serifs on the T. The lowercase e has an oblique bar to the eye, and the letter w has no middle serif. In the serif version, the A leans over to the right, and the letters v and w are narrow.

Dante

Dante was designed by Giovanni Mardersteig. His philosophy on designing and printing was to serve three purposes:

"First, service to the author, searching for the form best suited to his theme.

"Second, service to the reader, making reading as pleasant and light for him as possible.

"Third, the giving of the whole an attractive appearance without imposing too much self-will."

In 1954, Mardersteig created Dante, which was his last typeface that was cut. It appears to have been influenced by the Aldine types, though there are features that resemble some of the Venetian typefaces. It got its name from the book *Trattatello in Laude di Dante*, which Mardersteig printed in 1955. This typeface became Mardersteig's favorite and was used in the majority of books printed by him.

This typeface was originally a private-press type for the Officina Bodoni at Verona. As a book font, though, it is very crisp and clear, suited well for book paper as well as coated stocks. The height of the capitals falls slightly below that of the ascenders but not as noticeably as Bembo.

In 1955, the Monotype Corporation arranged to issue Dante to the public, using the 12-point size that was cut by Charles Malin. An italic chancery was also created to match the roman, and a titling face was created to go along with the typeface.

Futura

Futura has been called the face that expressed the "new typography" of its time. Futura was introduced in 1926 and was designed by Paul Renner, a book designer and founder of the Maters' School for German Printers in Munich.

226 DIGITAL TYPOGRAPHY POCKET PRIMER

The original design of Futura is what Renner felt each character would look like to the abstract thinker. In fact, without looking closely, some of the characters are not even recognizable. He sent the design to the Bauer Typefoundry of Frankfurt, which recommended some changes, and the face became what it is today.

In Futura, the M is splayed, the Q has a straight tail starting inside the bowl, and the T is narrow. The a is one story, the g has a unusual open tail, the t is square across the top, and the u is designed in the style of the uppercase.

Galliard
In 1978, the latest French old-style type, called Galliard, was introduced by the Mergenthaler Linotype Company. This typeface is based on the type made by the sixteenth century's Robert Granjon. This typeface was designed specifically for phototypesetting.

Galliard came from Granjon's term for an 8-point font cut about 1570. It refers to the style of the face, since galliard was a lively dance of the period, and the design of the face reflects this. Galliard possesses an authentic sparkle that is lacking in any versions of Garamond. This typeface is of solid weight, which brings excellent color to the page. The italic version is of a chancery style, which Garamond does not have. There are four weights for Galliard, including ultra and black.

Garamond
Claude Garamond was approached in the late 1520s to cut a new series of type. His typeface designs were based on those by Aldus Manutius. Garamond's first romans appeared in *Paraphrasis in Elegantiarum Libros Laurentii Vallae*. That year, many books were produced with Garamond's typeface.

Garamond died in 1561, and his equipment was sold, though soon many designers were creating variations of Garamond's typeface. In 1621, Jean Jannon showed his first specimen sheet. It was obvious, just by looking at the angle of the serifs on letters like the s, m, n, p, and r, that Jannon modeled his type after that of Garamond. The Jannon designs soon were forgotten and not used for about 200 years.

There are many other typeface versions that are models of the Garamond typeface by Jean Jannon as well as by Garamond himself.
These are:

- Deberny & Peignot, 1912-28. This design, supervised by
  Georges and later Charles Peignot, is based on the orig-
  inal types in the Imprimerie Nationale, which revived
  the Jannon types of 1641.
- American Type Founders, 1917, designed by M. F. Ben-
  ton and T. M. Cleland after the original Jannon types.
  Amsterdam Typefoundry, Linotype Garamond No. 3,
  and Intertype have been derived by ATF.
- Lanston Monotype, 1921, designed by F. W. Goudy after
  Jannon. The Monotype version follows Jannon in the ro-
  man and Granjon in the italic.
- Stempel, 1924. This design is based upon the Egenolff-
  Berner typographic specimen sheet. This design is avail-
  able on Linotypes.
- Mergenthaler Linotype, 1925, issued an adaptation by
  Joseph Hill. It is bolder and less closely set than the
  above version. This design is no longer available.
- Simoncini in Italy issued a Garamond font in 1958-61,
  designed by F. Simoncini and W. Bilz.

Granjon
Granjon is a modern recut of the original Garamond design. It was
produced under the supervision of George W. Jones for the Mergenthaler Linotype Company. The typeface was named after Robert Granjon, who was a punchcutter from 1545 to 1588.

When George Jones decided his company needed a Garamond, he
used the *Historia Eccasiastica* as a model. This version of Garamond
was a huge success as a book type, and the Merganthaler Company
quickly made it available to the American public.

Many stylistic characteristics make Granjon unique from other
typefaces. The middle strokes of the M are overhanging; the bowl
of the P is not closed; and the R ends in a foot serif on the line. As
well, the lowercase g with a small bowl is well reproduced. The
large bowl of the g is what separates this typeface from that of
Garamond.

Goudy Old Style

Frederic W. Goudy designed many typefaces that are still used today. After he had designed many typefaces that were for private use, the American Type Founders Company (ATF) spoke to Goudy about creating a typeface for them. He agreed, with the condition that his drawings would not be touched by the company's drawing room. With agreement from ATF, Goudy began working on Goudy Old Style by ATF, which became his most widely used typeface.

Goudy stated that the inspiration for Goudy Old Style came from a painting by Hans Holbein. One of the few regrets Goudy had about this typeface was the shortened descenders that he gave the characters. The short descenders, though, allowed commercial printers to economically use vertical spacing, which was important in advertising.

Goudy cut his own types, but several of the bold versions were designed by Morris F. Benton. It is the boldface version that has kept Goudy Old Style alive. Goudy once said that he wished he had designed the bold version, and drew a sketch of what it would look like, though it matched the version that Benton designed pretty closely.

Features of Goudy Old Style include the small serifs on the characters. The ear on the lowercase g projects upward, and the italics are upright. As stated earlier, the descenders are also shortened.

Goudy Text

Frederic W. Goudy created 126 type designs throughout his life. His most basic typeface was Goudy text, and it was developed midway through his creation of the other 122. In Marlborough, New York, Goudy established a type foundry, and it was there that he had realized that he had not designed any blackletter type designs. Goudy had created a blackletter that he called Goudy Black, and published it in his textbook *Elements of Lettering* in 1922.

The rest of this typeface was finished in 1928, and he started distributing it from Marlborough. Harvey Best, the president of the Lanston Monotype Machine Company, saw Goudy's typeface used in a Christmas card and wanted the cooperation of Goudy to make

Goudy Black into a Monotype Typeface, to be called Goudy Text. This typeface has become one of the most used of its kind in the United States.

To modern-day readers, blackletter fonts can be hard to follow because of the unfamiliar look to the letters. The capital letters were usually used as an initial letter and thus had many flourishes. To solve the problem, Goudy created a second set of capitals, based on the look of the initial caps created by the scribes. He called these Lombardic Capitals, and they were used as an alternative for the Goudy Text capital letters.

Goudy Text follows the appearance of the true textura letter of mid-fifteenth-century Italy. Textura is derived from the woven appearance of a page with blackletter type. The type is condensed and avoids all the excessive ornamentation that was applied to blackletter types.

After having created Goudy Text, Goudy admitted a typographic mistake of a tiny pointed projection at the left side of the stems of the letters b, h, k, and l. The spur belongs to the letter l, to distinguish it from the figure I.

Hammer Uncial
Victor Hammer in 1943 wrote, "With this uncial typeface, I am aiming at a letter form which eventually may fuse roman and blackletter, those two national letter forms, into a new unity. The impulse leading to this attempt came from a strong recognition of the difference between old and modern languages, as a fact which becomes obvious to anyone who tries, as I did, to write modern languages in an antique hand, acquired from the study of old manuscripts."

Hammer created the typeface American Uncial while attending Wells College in Aurora, New York. He liked the idea that the uncial was rounder and had a more open appearance than the blackletter fonts that were available. Hammer had some type cut for him, though he did not like or use the uncial typeface. He had observed the punchcutter's techniques and decided that he was going to cut his own type and create something he would feel comfortable using.

In 1939, Hammer returned to the United States from his home in Italy and was appointed to teach art and lettering at Wells College. This is when Hammer spent most of his time working on the typeface American Uncial. He cut the steel punches by hand and frantically looked for a founder who would cast his type for him. After Hammer looked for some time, Charles Nussbaumer of the Dearborn Type Foundry was chosen.

In the United States, no one was interested in selling Hammer's new Uncial typeface, so he returned to Europe, where it was produced for sale to both the United States and Europe. In America, this was the first typeface that allowed printers to create an authentic medieval feeling to their text. Soon the German Stempel foundry took over the foundry in Europe, and they changed the name of the font to Neue (new) Hammer Unziale.

In this font, serifs are long, thin, and flat, the g has an ear like that of Caslon, and the serifs in the italic version match those of roman typefaces.

Helvetica
Helvetica was designed by M. Miedinger, who followed the nineteenth-century style when designing the face. The type was formerly called Neue Haas Grotesk, for the Haas Typefoundry that released it in 1957. Later, Stempel and the Linotype Company recreated the font and rereleased it.

Helvetica is an example of a sans-serif typeface. It's a more geometric design than the humanist design of Gill Sans, but less geometric than Avant Garde and Futura. Helvetica is one of the few fonts that is improved by its bold version.

The a has a curved spur, and the tail of the Q is oblique.

Janson
The original font dates from about 1690 and was cut by Nicholas Kis, a Hungarian in Amsterdam. This was another type that was misnamed, since it was believed that it had been cut by Anton Janson. The original matrices have survived in Germany and since 1919 have been held at the Stempel foundry.

Book typographers were conscious of the fact that Caslon, unless firmly pressed into the page, was not dark enough. Also, when printed on coated stocks, Caslon created many problems. With Jenson, these problems were addressed, and it was made at a slightly heavier weight. Today, Janson is available from many sources. Experts in the field of typography consider the Stempel type foundry version the nicest, it being the original font. Herman Zapf has redesigned some of the weights and sizes for Stempel, basing the revisions on the original type.

Characteristics include the uppercase M, which is easily remembered because of its angles, and the lowercase g, with the curved ear. In the italic version, the m and n are squared up. As well, the v and w have curves for the apex and vertex.

Optima
Type designers had tried to create a sans-serif face for many years. In the United States, "gothic" became the term used for them, while in Europe they were known as "grotesque." In the 1920s, the sans-serif typefaces became a way to express oneself, though many of the designs were considered illegible.

In the 1950s, though, Herman Zapf created a sans serif that caught the eye of typographers around the world. This typeface became known as Optima. Zapf modeled his type after the sans-serif characters on the tombs in Florence's Santa Croce. In Optima, the capital letters have the proportions of the inscriptions found on the Trojan column. He then decided to try to create a face that would mix the roman structure with that of the sans serifs.

Then, in 1954 Zapf followed the suggestion of Monroe Wheeler from New York to try to adapt his face to be used as a book type. Zapf then went about changing the proportions of his designs and tested the reproduction of it.

Optima was first produced in 1958 by Stempel and after that by Merganthaler. Since then Optima had been produced under many names, Zapf wanted to call it New Roman, but his marketing staff insisted that it be called Optima. Not only did the face end up being used as a display face, it was designed to be used for body text as well. Optima is a sans serif with strokes thickened toward the end. The M is slightly splayed, and the g has Venetian form. Optima has been described as both a calligraphic roman or a modified sans serif.

Oxford

The Binney & Ronaldson typefoundry was the first commercially successful one in the United States. After a name change, they became MacKellar, Smiths, & Jordans and soon turned into the American Type Founders Company (ATF). One of the most successful typefaces that came from this typefoundry was originally called Roman No. 1.

Archibald Binney met James Ronaldson in Edinburgh, when Ronaldson's bakery burned down. At the time, Binney was looking for someone to start a typefoundry. Binny figured he would use his mechanical skills, and Ronaldson could use his business knowledge to start a company.

After trying to get their type out on the market with no luck with the first specimen book, they decided to do another. The second book, created in 1812, listed two roman types, with their italics, two blackletters, a Greek, a Hebrew, and four ornamental styles. The second typeface was Roman No.1.

This typeface was a transitional letter and has characteristics of old styles as well as some of the modern faces. Binny retired and sold the company to Ronaldson. Ronaldson soon created his own specimen book, and paid tribute to the work of Binny over the years. One characteristic of Binny's work was the elimination of the long s.

After 1822, the font known as Roman No. 1 slowly died. Seventy years later, Elihu White and David Bruce created specimen books and tried to revive the typeface. The face of White and Bruce could not match the delicate hand of Binny's, though, and no one would reproduce it until around 1898. John Cumming of Worcester, Massachusetts, was a punchcutter for the Dickinson Foundry and very capable of reproducing the work of Binney. Unfortunately, Roman No. 1 ended up in the ATF inventory, and the name was changed to Oxford.

Daniel Berkeley Updike expressed great enthusiasm for the Oxford face and used it in the book *Printing Types*. Updike felt that Caslon was too obtrusive and chose Oxford as his type of choice. Collectors can also look at the book *Early Printing in America* by the Grabhorns, published in 1921.

Palatino

In 1950, Hermann Zapf designed Palatino, which became well known throughout the world. The first book ever to be published in this typeface was *Feder und Stichel*. In 1951, Cooper Union recognized Zapf's talents and held an exhibition.

With this recognition, Zapf made his first trip to the United States and had the first English version of *Feder und Stichel* printed. Only 2,000 copies were produced and quickly sold out; they command high prices from booksellers today.

In 1950, Zapf also worked on a titling font to go along with Palatino and he called it Michelangelo. As well, two italics were created, one for the Linotype version and one for the single-type composition. The next addition was a bold titling font called Sistina, soon followed by a bold version of Palatino itself.

The open counters found in Palatino were meant to solve the problem of poor paper quality in Germany. The weight of the type was also thickened in order to be used in lithographic and gravure processes of the time. Without these features, the font would not have printed legibly.

If Zapf had had his own way, the font would have been named Medici. The type foundry decided, though, that it would be called Palatino, named after Giovanbattista Palatino, a sixteenth-century calligrapher.

Palatino achieved international status, although there was criticism of the endings of characters such as h, n, m, and the lowercase t. The capital M and W are wide, and the e has a large eye. As well, the g is wide, and the foot serifs on the final strokes of the h, m, and n are on the outside only. The lowercase y in the hot-metal font was made more ordinary in the phototypesetting fonts.

Sabon

In 1960, a group of printers decided to develop a typeface that could be made in identical versions of foundry type, Monotype, and Linotype. This new type also had to be legible and be able to be reproduced by any process. As well, the type had to resemble that of Garamond's early typefaces. German typographer Jan Tschihold ended up designing Sabon, which was no easy task. Tschihold had to get by the mechanical requirements of three very different methods of composition. The sources for the design are to be found on a specimen sheet of the Frankfurt typefounder Konrad Berner, who married the widow of Jacques Sabon, for whom the face is named.

Times Roman

Times Roman is the font that is typically used in today's computer-driven society. This font can be obtained from any source and is a standard among computer operating systems. Overall, Times Roman has become a universal typeface.

The design is credited to Stanley Morrison and Victor Lardent, who was an English typographic historian. In 1929, Lardent was asked to restyle the London newspaper called *The Times*. Morrison felt that the newspaper had not kept up with the mainstream and felt the type used needed to follow that of the book standards.

Times New Roman was the name of the type created for the reconstruction of the newspaper. Although Morrison was listed as the designer, he was not a craftsman and could not have have done it without help. On October 2, 1932, *The Times* was released with a new typeface and held all rights for the face for one year. This new font never caught on in the newspaper industry because *The Times* used whiter paper than other papers. With Times New Roman, it was impossible to print on dull stock that held more ink on a page. Though it never caught on in the newspaper industry, it did catch on in the commercial and book industries.

Currently, there is academic debate as to who actually created Times Roman.

10

Glossary
of Terms

Accents   A mark placed over, under, or through a character as a guide to pronunciation. In languages other than English, an accent refers to a mark that indicates a specific sound, stress, or pitch to distinguish the pronunciation of words, otherwise identically spelled.

Adobe Type Manager (ATM)   A software program or system extension manufactured by Adobe Systems that is used to enhance the display of screen fonts on computer monitors. Essentially, ATM uses the outline fonts (or printer fonts) rather than bitmap fonts, which not only allows for the creation of screen fonts in any type size but also reduces the memory and processing power needed for bitmaps. ATM also handles the downloading of fonts to a computer printer.

Alignment   A term used to refer to the proper positioning of all typefaces and size variations along an imaginary reference line. Alignment is a necessary consideration that ensures that all styles and sizes can be mixed in the same line.

Ampersand   A symbol used as an abbreviation of the word "and." Generally, a small-cap ampersand visually will look better used in company names and titles. Ampersands should never be used in continuous running text.

Apex   The part of a letter or other character where two stems meet at the top of a character, as in the point of the letter A.

Arm   The horizontal or diagonal stroke extending off the stem, as in the capital E.

Ascender   The portion of some lowercase letters that extends above the character's x-height.

ASCII   Abbreviation for American Standard Code for Information Interchange, pronounced "ASS-key," a file encoded in the industry-standard representation for text. ASCII is a set of standard codes used by most computers to symbolize letters, numbers, punctuation, and sets of commands (such as returns, etc.) but not style attributes, such as bold, italic, or other formatting commands. The ASCII standard character set of a microcomputer usually includes 256 characters or control codes. A "plain ASCII" file can be read by just about any program. Files created in a word-processing, page-makeup, or other type of program are often translated to and saved as an ASCII file (often called a text file) for transmitting via modem. Text saved in ASCII can be opened in virtually any word-processing program of page-makeup software.

Asterisk   A pi character used in footnotes and references. It is also used as a wild-card character in many computerized search engines.

Ballot box   A box or circle, usually possessing a drop shadow, used in bulleted lists or checklists.

Bar   An arm of a letter or other character connected to a stroke on both sides, as in the letter H.

Bézier curves   In computer graphics, a smooth, mathematically defined curve or line defined by two endpoints (called anchor points) and two control points (called Bézier control points) in a region adjacent to the curve.

Bitmap   In computer graphics, the collection of individual data—or pixels—that makes up a screen image. Bitmapped or raster images are defined as a series of dots. The edges of bitmaps tend to exhibit a stairstep pattern known as aliasing. Output resolution is limited by the size of the pixel matrix.

Blackletter   One of a wide variety of typefaces based on medieval script, commonly from thirteenth-century German writing. This style is characterized by dark, angular characters comprising thick and thin lines.

Boldface   A type style characterized by heavier weight than the "plain" versions of the characters. The primary use for bold characters is for emphasis or headlines.

Bowl   The curved stroke of a letter or other character which creates an enclosed space in the character, as in the stroke that forms the center of the letter e. A complete bowl is formed by only one curved stroke, while a modified bowl has the stem forming one of the sides.

Bracket   Descriptive of the curvature linking the main vertical stem of a letter to the horizontal serif. A slight curvature between the stem and serif is known as fine bracketing, while a pronounced curvature is known as full.

B-spline   A continuous curve defined by a series of control points. The curve is formed in relation to a line joining the points in sequence. The B-spline curve always starts at the first control point and ends at the last control point, and it is always tangent to the polyline at these end points, but in general it does not pass through the other control points. It is shaped by them into a continuous line. Thus a few points can define a complex shape, such as a typographic glyph.

Bullet   A common type pi character used for decorative purposes. Bullets should be close to the x-height of the text they accompany. Bullets are also used to delineate and emphasize points or examples. They are either open or closed. A widely used example is a ballot box.

Cap height   The height of a capital letter measured from the baseline to the top of the letter.

Character   Any letter, number, punctuation mark, or other symbol that is typeset.

Character map   On the Windows platform, the character map is used to show what characters are available in a typeface and which keys to enter to make them appear on the screen.

Color   In the typographic sense, *color* refers to the overall shade of gray perceived by the eye. Color can be interrupted by bad word breaks or character spacing, as well as uneven leading.

Column   A vertical area of running text on a page. In page-layout software, text that spans the entire width of a page is considered a column, although a column is conventionally thought of as some fractional division of a page. The width of a column should be based on type size and legibility, and is a factor of line length.

Condensed   Descriptive of the relative narrowness of all the characters in one typeface. Condensed type is used when large amounts of copy need to fill a small space, as in tabular composition.

Counter   The space in a letter or other character that is enclosed—either fully or partially—by the strokes of the character.

Crossbar   A horizontal stroke that passes through the stem.

Dagger   A pi character used in footnotes and references. The single dagger is the second reference mark after the asterisk.

Descender   The portion of a lowercase letter that extends below the character's x-height. They may not always align at the bottom of the descender, although most do. Descenders in one typeface may be shorter or longer than another, depending on the style and mood the typeface was created to express.

Didot system   A unit (corps) used predominantly in continental Europe to measure type. One Didot point equals 0.0148 inches; 12 Didot corps equal 1 cicero. The Didot point is slightly larger than the point used in the English system, which equals 0.0138 inches.

Diphthong   A combination of two vowels pronounced as a single sound and typeset as a single character.

Dithering   Using the values of two pixels to determine the color of a pixel lying between them. This new pixel thus has a value that is the average of the two pixels on either side of it. Dithering is used to eliminate unwanted jaggies or to determine the value of certain pixels when reducing the color depth of an image.

Dot matrix   Any grid pattern of dots that makes up an image. A dot matrix can refer to nearly any digital output or display device. The term is commonly used to refer to a type of computer printer popular before the advent of inexpensive laser and inkjet printers.

Dots per inch (DPI)   A measure of the resolution of a computer monitor, scanner, or output device such as a laser printer or imagesetter. Each of these devices generates or displays images composed of tiny dots. The resolution is determined by measuring how many of these dots can fit in a unit of linear distance, such as an inch.

Double dagger   A pi character used in footnotes and references. The double dagger is the third reference mark after asterisk and single dagger.

Download   To receive a data file on one's computer from another computer. Typically, downloads are done over modems, though they can be done using faster media such as T-3 lines.

Downloadable font   In computers and desktop publishing systems, a digital font that can be sent to an output device from the computer's hard disk and loaded into the printer's memory, as opposed to a font that needs to be stored in a plug-in cartridge.

Drop caps   A large letter—typically the first letter of the first word of the line—placed at the beginning of a chapter, page or paragraph. The oldest style is the sunken initial, in which the initial letter is set down within the copy, not rising above the top line of the text. The second style is the raised initial, or stickup initial, in which the initial letter rests on the baseline of the first or subsequent line of text and rises above the top line of the text.

Drop shadow   Shaded typefaces that are designed with a third dimension. This type lends itself to two-color display applications.

Ear   A short stroke extending off the stem, bowl, or other portion of a letter or other character, such as the small protuberance from the bowl of a lowercase g.

Ellipsis   The three periods used to indicate that something is missing or that a conversation has stopped. An ellipsis is commonly set open. If the ellipsis occurs at the end of a sentence, and the sentence is complete, the period is set closed to the last character, followed by the three ellipsis points.

Em   A fixed space having a height and a width equal to the point size.

Em dash   A dash equal to the size of an em space in a particular typeface at a particular size. It is used to set off parenthetical text, replace missing text, or function in lieu of a colon.

En   A unit of measurement exactly one-half as wide and as high as the point size being set.

En dash   A dash as wide as the en space for a particular typeface and type size. It is used to replace the words "to" or "through" in a range and also to connect two nouns of equal weight or to replace a colon.

Ending   The final stroke of a character that could include a serif, terminal, swash, eye, spur, counter, finial, etc.

EPS   Encapsulated PostScript, a graphics file format developed by Adobe Systems, Inc. The EPS format is a device-independent PostScript representation of a graphic or other object. It stores files not only as a series of Bézier curves but also includes a low-resolution bitmap representation of the file for quick on-screen viewing.

Expanded   Descriptive of the relative wideness of all the characters in one typeface. Expanded type is used in heads, subheads, and some ad copy.

Expert set   A font containing a set of accents, small caps, fractions, and other specialized characters, in addition to the basic character set.

Figures   A term used to refer to numerals. The numbers 1 through 0 come in two versions: old-style figures and lining figures. One set of figures used throughout the world is known as arabic numerals; another form still used is called Roman numerals.

Finale   On a character, the tapering end of a stroke.

Fixed space   A blank space of a fixed increment, used where a consistent-width blank space is required, since typographic word spaces vary in width according to the justification needs of a line. The common widths are the em, en, and thin spaces.

Folios   A page number, commonly placed outside the running head at the top of a page. Folios are commonly set flush left on verso (left) pages and flush right on recto (right) pages. They can be set centered at the top of the page instead. A folio that appears on the bottom of a page is known as a *drop folio*. A folio counted in page numbering but not actually printed is called a *blind folio*, and a printed folio is known as an *expressed folio*.

Font   A set of all characters in a typeface. A type font contains all the alphanumeric, punctuation marks, special characters, ligatures, etc., contained in a typeface.

Font folder   A folder that exists on both the Macintosh and PC platforms in which the font files are stored.

Footnotes   A reference relating to the main body of text, positioned at the bottom of the page. Footnotes are referenced by certain symbols, letters, or numbers, most often in superior or superscript form. The footnote always begins on the same page as its reference but may be carried over at the bottom of successive pages. A short rule or additional space should separate the footnote from the text. The first line of the footnote is normally indented; some are set flush left. The point size of a footnote should be either 7 or 8 point.

Formats   Any combination of point size, line spacing, line length, typeface, placement, and style that contributes to producing a specific typographic appearance.

Fractions A numeric symbol indicating a portion of a whole number. A fraction is made up of a numerator, denominator, and a dividing line. There are several types of fractions including the em, en, piece, fake, and decimal fractions. Type-font suppliers often substitute fractions from one typeface for others that are closely related. It is important to ensure that the fraction fits the typeface in weight and design.

Geometric figures Typeface classification of sans serifs constructed on simple geometric shapes.

Glyph Any pictogram used to convey information. A glyph is also a coding system used in computing that utilizes printed symbols. After scanning, these symbols are converted into data by the computer. A bar code is a type of glyph.

Grayscale Shades of gray from black to white. Grayscales are used to analyze and optimize the contrast of color and black-and-white images. A grayscale can be supplied on film, as either continuous tones or halftone dots. On a monitor, grayscales are produced by varying the intensity of the pixels, on a scale of white to black. Images saved in TIFF formats convert grayscale information into printer commands, which instruct the printer to construct a bitmap, plotting the levels of gray for each spot in the output. The more levels of gray, the smoother and more realistic the image will look.

Hairline rule A very thin rule, typically less than 0.5 points wide. On some output devices, the hairline rule is the smallest printer spot the device can image. On 600-PPI (pixels per inch) laser printers, the hairline rule is effective; however, on high-resolution (2,400+ PPI) imagesetters, it can be essentially invisible.

Head Display type used to emphasize copy; act as a book, chapter, or section title; or otherwise introduce separate text.

Hints A variety of algorithms—such as those encrypted in Type 1 PostScript fonts—that improve the appearance of characters, especially those in small sizes, by rendering screen fonts more uniformly shaped across the set of characters.

Homophone Words that are spelled the same but pronounced and hyphenated differently according to use, such as pro-cess (verb, with a long o) and proc-ess (noun, with a short o). Computer programs that hyphenate automatically cannot handle homophones, because the meanings between words cannot be discerned.

HTML   Stands for hypertext markup language, used on the World Wide Web. HTML is a standard language used to create Web pages and other hypertext-based documents. An HTML document creates text as well as codes corresponding to linked files, which can be graphics, video, audio, or other pages. Since HTML is a markup language and not a program, any program capable of producing text can be used to create a Web page, although there are a number of programs that make the creation of a Web page easier. Many desktop publishing programs now feature the ability to add HTML coding to documents, allowing pages to be prepared for print and electronic distribution.

Humanist typeface   This type classification refers to typefaces with wide, square proportions. As well, there is little contrast between strokes. The distinguishing factor between this class and most others is the distinctive slant to the bar of the lowercase e.

Hyphen   A very small dash used to break words or syllables at the ends of lines, or to connect parts of compound or connected words.

Hyphenation   The breaking of a word into syllables and inserting hyphens manually or automatically, so that the word remains consistent —within prescribed limits—for proper justification. A discretionary hyphen is inserted in a word during input to give the system a specific point to hyphenate, and that point will take precedence over any logic-generated point. Hyphenation is often considered together with justification.

Indents   The positioning of the text of one or more lines at fixed distances from one or both margins of a page. The most common is the *paragraph indent*, which is an indentation of the first line of a paragraph. A *hanging indent* has the first line set flush with the left (or right) margin, while the rest of the lines are indented. A *runaround indent* is the indentation of a certain number of lines to make room for an illustration or other page element. Finally, a *skewed indent* is a varied indenting of subsequent lines, giving the margin a slanted appearance.

Inferior   Characters set in a smaller point size and positioned below the baseline. Also called *subscript*. Inferiors are used for chemical equations. They are most often numerals, but letters can be used. Inferiors can be manufactured by changing to a smaller size and adjusting the baseline.

Initial caps   *See* Drop caps.

Italic   A variation in the posture of the characters in a particular typeface, specifically, a slant to the right. Today, italic type is used for emphasis, or in the setting of the titles of books, movies, etc.

Justification Setting multiple lines of type so that they will line up on the left and right, as opposed to ragged right, in which the lines do not line up on the right.

Kerning The reduction (or addition) of letterspace between characters to reduce the space between them, performed for aesthetic reasons. Typeset characters have specific width values and are positioned within an imaginary rectangle. In the process of kerning, the space is reduced or increased by "fooling" the typesetting equipment. Most computer typesetting systems can kern more than 200 character pairs automatically. Kerning is essentially an optical function in which space between characters is decreased until it optically looks right. Another term for kerning is *negative letterspacing*.

Key Caps On the Macintosh platform, the Key Caps feature allows the user to see what characters are available for various fonts and how to access them.

Leaders Dots or dashes that lead the eye from one side of a line to the other. Hairline rules under type can sometimes replace leaders. Regular leaders, in dot or hyphen style, are set in two, four, or six dots to the em. The period is most often used as a leader, though it may look better if the point size is increased.

Leading (Pronounced "ledding.") An alternate and more popularly used term for line spacing. It is derived from the strips of flat metal, usually made of lead, that were used to space lines of metal type.

Legibility The ease with which typeset copy is read. Legibility deals with how we read and how the eye fixates on something each quarter of a second and takes in a group of words. It then jumps to the next fixation. Legibility has been reflected in the design of letterforms. Large x-height serif faces with a bolder print to them tend to score highly in legibility research. For optimum legibility, letterspacing should be the width of the lowercase i, and leading should be slightly larger than the word space. Research has also found that narrower line lengths, consistent word spacing, upper- and lowercase lettering, and well-designed typefaces aid in efficient reading.

Letterspacing The space between letters or other characters. There are two variations: negative and positive letterspacing. *Positive letterspacing* is adding additional space between characters, while *negative* is the subtracting of space equally from between all letters in small units.

Ligature Two or more characters designed as a distinct unit and commonly available as a single character.

Line length   The overall width of a typeset line, usually the area between two margins. Also called *measure, column width,* or *line measure.* There are several rules for establishing the line length. Wider typefaces look best with wider line lengths; condensed faces look best with narrow line lengths. In most cases, instead of wide line lengths in a single column, double or multiple columns of smaller line length should be used.

Lining figures   A style of numeral in which all the numerals align with each other at the top and bottom and are commonly the same height as the capital letters of a given typeface.

Link   The short stroke that joins the bowl of the lowercase g to its loop.

Logotypes   A symbol representing a company or product. Today, a logotype is usually a specific designed company name. A logo is a design that emphasizes typography, in contrast to a symbol, which is usually an abstract, nontypographic image. Logotypes and symbols are usually included in special pi fonts.

Loop   The part of the letter or other character consisting of a bowl that serves as a flourish, as in the bottom portion of the lowercase g.

Macintosh   A type of personal computer manufactured by Apple Computer, distinguished primarily by its use of the Mac OS. It was introduced in 1984 and was a direct descendant of an earlier Apple device called the Lisa, which in turn was derived from a primitive graphical user interface devised by Xerox at its Palo Alto Research Center in the 1970s. The Macintosh is also distinguished by its ease of use. The PowerMac is the latest line of Macintosh computers and boasts increasingly fast performance as well as the ability to run Microsoft Windows files and programs.

Mac OS   The Macintosh Operating System. This system controls all computer functions, from finding files to opening applications, formatting external media, etc. This was the first graphical user interface; its ease of use and "what you see is what you get" display helped popularize desktop publishing.

Mediaan system   Once used principally in Belgium, the Mediaan system has a corps equal to 0.01374 inches. The Mediaan em, or cicero, measures 0.165 inches. This system has largely been replaced by the Didot system.

Modern typefaces   Typeface classification in which the characters are narrow with an extreme contrast between stroke widths and letters. The extreme thick and thin strokes make some typefaces in this class strictly for display purposes.

Multiple master A means—developed by Adobe Systems—of describing outline fonts in terms of weight, width, and style, each aspect of which comprises a sliding scale between extremes. The user can thus adjust any or all of those characteristics.

Oblique An alternate term for *italic*, descriptive of a right-leaning change in the posture of the characters in a particular typeface. Although "oblique" can refer to any italic version of a typeface, it is often used to describe a matching italic face, or an italic created by merely shifting the angle of the roman characters electronically.

Old-style figures A style of figures in which certain numerals have ascenders and descenders, in contrast to lining figures, in which all digits align on the baseline.

Old-style typefaces A typeface design that dates from the early day of printing, specifically those utilized by Venetian printers in the late fifteenth century, or type styles derived from those early styles. Such faces are characterized by variations in stroke and width, bracketed serifs, and diagonal strokes.

OpenType The OpenType font format is an extension of the TrueType font format, adding support for PostScript font data. The OpenType font format was developed jointly by Microsoft and Adobe. OpenType fonts and the operating system services that support OpenType fonts provide users with a simple way to install and use fonts, whether the fonts contain TrueType outlines or CFF (PostScript) outlines.

Optical alignment Involves the use of visual reference points. It may require that the curved or angular characters be placed slightly off the baseline to achieve the proper look.

Optical spacing The "look" of the typeset letters in relation to each other, which may or may not be geometrically accurate due to optical illusions caused by the proximity of various letter shapes. In good typeface design, spacing between lowercase letters is built in.

Orphans A single line of a new paragraph or column that falls at the bottom of a page or column.

Outline A typeface with no "insides." Outline faces are used in display work and lend themselves to colored or tinted layouts, allowing the type to drop out of the background. The letters can be used for special effect in color or dropout of color. Since these are "busy" typefaces, they should be used sparingly and only in display sizes.

Pagination The assembly of type into pages. *Typesetting* is the process of setting type; *pagination* is the process of putting pages together with that type and other graphic elements. The basic building blocks are text blocks, display lines, line illustrations, photographs, captions, footnotes, tabular blocks, and page numbers. The term *pagination* can also refer to the process of numbering pages.

Parenthesis Used in pairs except when enumerated divisions are paragraphed. A single parenthesis is ordinarily used to follow a lowercase letter or a lowercase roman numeral. Parentheses enclose information that may be a side thought or that helps to clarify preceding information.

PC Stands for personal computer but is also used to describe an IBM-compatible computer. In these terms, it describes any computer not made by IBM that is compatible with IBM software. PCs usually use either MS-DOS or Microsoft Windows as an operating system. These are the most commonly used computers.

PDF Stands for Portable Document Format. It's a distribution format developed by Adobe Corporation to allow electronic information to be transferred between various types of computers. The software that allows this transfer is called Acrobat. In order to view and print one of our PDF files, you will first need to download and install a copy of the Adobe Acrobat Reader. Adobe Portable Document Format (PDF) is the open de facto standard for electronic document distribution worldwide. PDF is a universal file format that preserves all of the fonts, formatting, colors, and graphics of any source document, regardless of the application and platform used to create it. PDF files are compact and can be shared, viewed, navigated, and printed exactly as intended by anyone.

Pica A basic unit of measurement in typography. One pica equals 12 points, and 6 picas equal approximately 1 inch. The term pica also refers to a 10-pitch typewriter font.

Pi fonts A collection of special characters, such as mathematics, fractions, monetary symbols, or decorative symbols. A type manufacturer can create customized pi fonts for special needs, and new software programs allow for the easy creation of special digital fonts. Special fonts were developed for television listings, for instance.

Pixels Shorthand term for picture element, or the smallest point or dot on a computer monitor. Any computer display is divided into rows and columns of tiny dots, which are individual points at which the scanning electron beam has hit the phosphor-coated screen. The pixel is the smallest indivisible point of display on a monitor.

Point size   A measure of the height of the characters of a font, measured in points. The point is the basic unit of measurement used in typography, and all other measurements are derived from it. In the late nineteenth century, the point system—devised a century earlier by Pierre Fournier—was adopted by the printing industry.

Point system   A measurement system used in typography. The system dates from early handset type, where the sizes of type cast founders were graduated on a uniform point scale. Each size is described by its number of points, which referred to the height of the body on which it is cast. The standard of measurement is the 0.166-inch pica and the 0.01383-inch point.

PostScript   A page-description language invented by Adobe Systems, consisting of software commands that, when translated through a RIP, form the desired image on an output device. PostScript is commonly used for both text and line art. In the latter case, it is often referred to as Encapsulated PostScript (EPS). PostScript allows for device independence, or the ability to generate virtually identical output on devices made by different manufacturers, as long as they can interpret PostScript commands.

Prime mark   A short vertical stroke positioned along the cap line. A single prime is used to identify feet, while the double prime mark identifies inches. The double prime is appropriate in tables, charts, and technical or informal writing; in most text uses, "inches" and "feet" should be spelled out.

Printer font   A computer file—either in PostScript format or other page-description language format—containing mathematical descriptions or image outlines of a particular typeface. Printer fonts can be downloaded to the printer and called up when a document utilizing a particular font is sent to the printer. Most fonts available for computers contain printer fonts, which, being vector-based rather than bitmapped, ensure that the output is at a high resolution.

Proportional width   Individual character-width relationships based on character shape and typeface design.

Pull quotes   In magazine publishing (and occasionally elsewhere), a small extract of text from a story or article and set off from the main text, often in a larger point size and/or different typeface and surrounded by a border or rule. Often a pull quote is used for emphasis.

Punctuation   Symbols used to break up or end sentences, such as the period, comma, question mark, exclamation point, apostrophe, and quotation marks.

Quadratic Another term for B-spline. *See* B-spline.

QuarkXPress A popular page-makeup program developed by Quark, Inc., widely used to assemble page elements—from text to line art and halftones—for output to a laser printer, imagesetter, or other device. QuarkXPress also allows for the specification of spot color or desktop color separation. QuarkXPress is available for both the Macintosh and Windows platforms.

QuickDraw GX Apple's new imaging technology, QuickDraw GX, enables applications to provide users with fonts having special typographical effects, such as cursive connection, ornateness, and complex ligatures. Many of these features are required for scripts, such as Arabic or Devanagari. Font vendors can create tables that implement different sets of features. Applications can pick and choose your font to determine the features available. The font tables store sets of strings identifying the features that can be presented to the user.

Quotes The opening and closing punctuation marks indicating verbal statements or defining or emphasizing certain words. Double quotes are normally used in American books, with single quotes being used within double quotes, if needed. In Great Britain, the style is reversed.

RAM Abbreviation for random-access memory. RAM is essentially the working memory a computer uses to store the temporary information. RAM can be read from and written to, as its name indicates, in a random sequence, and is used to store data from open applications as well as the operating system itself. The RAM is cleared or emptied when the power is turned off. RAM is housed on memory chips or boards and can be expanded by adding more. A computer accesses RAM much faster than it can access a hard drive or any external media.

Raster image processor In computer graphics and imaging, the hardware and software configuration used in output devices to determine what value each pixel or spot of output should possess, driven by commands from a page-description language such as PostScript. Computer-generated output is composed of very small spots. The RIP converts a vector-based image, or an image (such as type or line art), stored by the computer as a series of mathematical formulas that describe lines and curves, into the pattern of spots needed to generate the output.

Readability All typographic decisions determine readability. If the reader becomes confused, tired, or discouraged while reading a document, the message is not delivered. When continuous text is set in all capital letters, it will lower readability, since there are no descenders to differentiate the letters and words from one another. Other things that help to add or take away from readability include paper stock, type style, and reading patterns.

Resolution A measure to the extent to which the human eye can distinguish between the smallest discrete parts of an image. In terms of human vision, though, this is more or less a subjective measurement, due to the variability among individuals in how well their eyes can resolve small images. Output resolution is measured in lines per inch (LPI), since many times dots cannot be measured easily in an inch because of overlap. Pixels per inch (PPI) is also used and is the measurement of choice for most output and input device specifications. As a general rule, the higher the resolution, the better (though if the printer can only handle 2,400 PPI, it makes no sense to scan an image at 3,300 PPI).

Roman numerals The style of numeral used exclusively until about the tenth century A.D., originally used by the Romans. They are typeset just as capital letters are. The front matter of most books is paginated using lowercase Roman numerals.

Rule Used for horizontal ruling, including underlining. A rule is an em-width dash, repeated to form a line. The lightest rule is called a hairline, and following that is the half-point rule, 1-point rule, and up from there by increments of 1 point.

Runaround Copy set so that it will create a "hole" on the page that fits around an illustration, photo, or other page element.

Running feet In book typography, a "heading"—such as a book title, chapter title, or author—that is located at the bottom of consecutive pages and may contain a folio.

Running head In book typography, a "heading"—such as a book title, chapter title, or author—that is located at the top of consecutive pages and may contain a folio.

Sans serif Characters without serifs crossing the free end of the stroke. In the United States, the term "gothic" was sometimes used as a synonym. In Europe, it is sometimes referred to as "grotesque." Most sans-serif typefaces have a neutral feeling, though some have touches of serifs included in some of their characters. The most popular sans-serif typefaces today have a calligraphic feel to them.

Scaling The act of—or the computer function that facilitates—altering a font proportionately, vertically or horizontally.

Screen fonts   A computer file containing bitmap outlines of a particular typeface, used to display that font on the computer monitor. As bitmaps, screen fonts occasionally look fine and legible at the resolution of the computer screen but are too low in resolution for high-quality typographic output.

Serifs   An all-inclusive term for characters that have a line crossing the free end of a stroke. The term "serif" refers to both the finishing line and to character typefaces that have them.

Shoulder   A curved stroke forming part of a letter.

Slab serif   A serif character or typeface characterized by serifs that are as heavy or heavier than the bodies of the letters and that have no curvature between the main stroke and the serif.

Small caps   Capital letters designed to match the x-height of a particular typeface and size. Since many fonts do not have small caps, they are created by reducing the point size by two sizes (or three-quarters the font size) and setting capital letters. Expert fonts include true small caps, which are the right weight to match the typeface.

Solidus   A slanted line used to create fractions, or separate one type character from another. Also called a *shilling, virgule, fraction bar*, or *slash*.

Spacing   Any fixed- or variable-width regions separating one character, word, or line from another.

Spine   The main curved stroke of the capital or lowercase S.

Spur   A letter element corresponding to a small projection off a main stroke, such as that found on many capital Gs.

Stem   The primary, straight vertical stroke of a letter or other character, or the primary diagonal stroke in an oblique character.

Stroke   The primary line or curve making up a letter or other character.

Style sheet   In electronic publishing systems and page-makeup software, a set of type formats that can be stored and applied to blocks of text, eliminating the need to re-create the type characteristics from scratch each time a format change needs to be made.

Superior   Characters set in a smaller point size and positioned above the baseline. Also called a *superscript*. Superior characters are used for exponents, footnotes, etc. They are most often numerals, but letters can be used as well. Superiors can be manufactured by changing to a smaller size and adjusting the baseline. Superiors align at the cap height or the ascender height, and most systems position them automatically.

Swash   A set of letters—loosely based on italics—but with elaborate flourishes, tails, ascenders, and descenders.

Symbols   *See* Pi font.

Tab   A column in which type—usually tabular material—is to be arranged, or the keyboard key used to jump to start points of columns.

Tabular   A vertical alignment within multiple columns. A combination of en spaces and thin spaces is used to line up tabular material. Depending on the nature of the columns, alignment may be consistent or inconsistent.

Tail   The downward-sloping short stroke on a letter or other character ending free.

Terminal   The free-ending stroke of a letter or other character, commonly with a special decorative treatment.

Thin space   A small fixed space equal in width to a comma or period.

Tracking   Universal letterspacing. *See* Letterspacing.

Trapping   The compensation for misregister of successive colors or images. Trapping ensures that there are no unsightly gaps or overlaps of successively printed colors or images.

TrueType   A type of computer font format created by Apple Computer as an alternative to Adobe PostScript fonts. TrueType fonts can be used both for bitmapped screen display and for vector-based output, the goal being to eliminate the need for two sets of fonts: screen fonts and printer fonts. Systems cannot utilize both TrueType fonts and fonts running with Adobe Type Manager (ATM).

Type classification   A system that categorizes type by characteristics of the typeface itself. There are many different classification systems in use in the world today.

Typeface   A specific version within a type family, such as roman, italic, bold, etc. In other words, the basic design of the type combined with the weight characteristics and the width characteristics.

Type families   A group of typefaces created with common design characteristics. Each member may vary by weight and width and may have related italic versions.

Typography   The art and process of specifying, setting, or otherwise working with print-quality type, as opposed to typewriting. Typography involves the proper placement, positioning, and specification of type to ensure not only maximum legibility but also high aesthetic appeal.

Uncial typeface   A type of modified majuscule letterform. Uncials are biform characters making the transition from caps to lowercase as scribes tried to write faster and faster. The progression continued through the half-uncial letterform to the Caroline minuscule.

Underline   Originally used in typewriting for emphasis and to indicate the equivalent of italic. Underlining should be a design decision, and creativity should never override clarity. Underlining should go behind the descenders, not through them.

White space   The total amount of nonimage area on a page, particularly gutters and margins. White space also refers to the space on either side of typographic characters, that can be reduced with tracking.

Widows   The last line of a paragraph when it is less than one-third the width of the line, especially when it is the carryover of a hyphenated word. Widow can also refer to one word or word part standing alone in a line of a heading or caption. A single line of a paragraph or column that falls at the top of a page or column is also considered a widow. Widows are undesirable and can be eliminated by adding or deleting words to or from the previous line to either fill out the widow line or remove it entirely. Adjusting the set width and tracking of the line can also eliminate the occurrence of widows.

x-height   The height of the lowercase letter x, representing the most important area of a letterform for 90% of lowercase characters. A character's x-height does not take into account ascenders or descenders and is thus a more realistic measurement of the size of a typeface than point size.

Index